99364

LOCKHEED
STEALTH

BILL SWEETMAN

MBI Publishing Company

First published in 2001 by MBI Publishing Company, Galtier Plaza, Suite 200, 380 Jackson Street, St. Paul, MN 55101-3885, USA

MBI Publishing Company books are also available at discounts in bulk quantity for industrial or sales-promotional use. For details write to Special Sales Manager at Motorbooks International Wholesalers & Distributors, Galtier Plaza, Suite 200, 380 Jackson Street, St. Paul, MN 55101-3885, USA.

Library of Congress Cataloging-in-Publication Data Available

ISBN 0-7603-0852-7

On the front cover
The F-22 Raptor is the first aircraft to combine low-observable technology with the gut-wrenching agility needed for an air superiority fighter. Prior to the F-22, an aircraft could have stealth or maneuverability, but not both.

On the frontispiece
The X-35 full-scale mockup mounted atop a 40-foot tower at Lockheed's high-fidelity sensor integration facility. Here the X-35's sensor subsystems are tested to ensure their smooth integration with the overall avionics package. *Lockheed Martin*

On the title page
The X-35A in flight test. The JSF prototypes have three principal tasks: to demonstrate the basic aerodynamics of the design, to show that the carrier-based version meets basic Navy requirements and to demonstrate the STOVL performance of the Marine version. *Lockheed Martin*

On the back cover
The Lockheed Martin X-35A runs up its engine in preparations for its first flight. All four JSF prototypes–Boeing's X-32s and Lockheed's X-35s–have Pratt & Whitney F119 engines, specially modified to suit their STOVL systems. *Lockheed Martin*

Edited by Mike Haenggi
Designed by Katie Sonmor

Printed in Hong Kong

contents

dedication

To Martin Sweetman and Sarah Niemann, aspiring aerospace engineers.

"There is nothing more difficult to take in hand, more perilous to conduct, or more
uncertain in its success, than to take the lead in the introduction of a new order of
things. Because the innovator has for enemies all those who have done well under
the old conditions, and lukewarm defenders
in those who may do well under the new."

— *Machiavelli*

acknowledgments

Any book is the work of many people other than the one whose name
appears on the cover. I would like to mention four of the pioneers of
stealth—Alan Brown, Denys Overholser, Irv Waaland, and John Cashen—for
giving their time in interviews that provide this book with much of its content.

Thanks are also due to Eric Hehs and Denny Lombard of Lockheed
Martin, and to Chris Pocock, for their help with illustrations.

Twenty years ago, in 1981, I moved from the United Kingdom to California with my wife, Mary Pat, and a few large crates containing our possessions, including a manual typewriter. A few months later, using that typewriter, I summed up in a four-page article for *New Scientist* what the unclassified world knew about stealth.

What a long, strange trip it's been.

Typewriters are collectibles and text and pictures fly around the world at light speed. Meanwhile, in a slow, cumbersome and fitful process, stealth technology has come out of the shadows, and those of us who wrote about it in its early days have been able to check some of our guesses against reality. Some strange stories have remained in the unconfirmed file. Others turned out to be surprisingly true (such as the outlandish idea of draping a U-2 in a framework of wire). It has been a useful lesson in the importance of keeping an open mind, being ready to reevaluate what you think you know, and maintaining the discipline to refrain from dismissing anything out of hand.

In 1997, I spoke to a conference in the United Kingdom on stealth. My title, paraphrasing Will Rogers, was "Ten Important Things That You Know About Stealth That Ain't So." For example, people think that stealth aircraft are designed on computers. Today, all aircraft are designed on computers, but stealth aircraft, more than most, demand some serious use of the computer located between the designer's ears. Aircraft design alone is not the key to stealth; there is no magic that will make up for good test facilities and the sensible balance of technology and tactics.

Some planners believe that stealth is too expensive to be an option for some missions. There is no denying that the stealth aircraft developed so far have been expensive, but in many cases that is because of other requirements, unrelated to stealth. The story of the A-12 would have been very different, had the customer not demanded a B-29-like internal weapon load.

Myths are sometimes originated by the uninformed, sometimes by people with personal or institutional stakes in the debate, and sometimes out of mere malice. Usually, truth bests myth in the marketplace of ideas. It hasn't happened that way with stealth, much of the time for one reason: security.

The veil of secrecy that was cast over stealth in 1975 served its purpose. There is every sign that the Soviet Union's technical intelligence services failed to assess the extent to which U.S. engineers had succeeded in reducing radar cross-section until the mid-to-late-1980s.

But the penalty of secrecy was the expansion of a surreal, paranoid parallel-world that had hitherto existed only in the black chambers of the world's intelligence agencies. As it was in Stalin's Russia, everything is secret and the price of being too talkative is too high to risk. Secrets are kept for no apparent reason. What is the harm of identifying Area 51, when it is visible on a dozen satellite databases and thousands of Internet sites? Why are old programs such as Senior Prom, Quartz, and the Lockheed stealth bomber design still concealed from view? The rules are so irrational that only a few people in the stealth world have felt comfortable telling their stories face to face, without a PR watchdog on hand.

Consequently, misinformation often went unchallenged. The opponents of stealth had free run of the media and Capitol Hill, and they used their influence to cut back production of the B-2 and delay the F-22. Navy program managers used the secrecy surrounding the stealthy A-12 in an attempt to beat the Air Force to the pot of procurement funds. The results have been disastrous: even the ill-fated A-12, with its unique balance of self-defense and stealth, was better than it seemed at the time.

What use is secrecy, if it denies the benefits of technology to your own forces as well as to your enemy?

—Bill Sweetman

Chapter 1

STEALTH
BEFORE STEALTH

Who invented Stealth? This is not quite as dumb or simplistic a question as you might think, given our modern historical tendency to spread both credit and guilt as broadly as we can, and to attribute both good and bad actions and ideas to seismic social and economic forces.

Stealth was, indeed, invented rather than discovered. Had you polled the world's most eminent designers of military aircraft in 1970, it is a safe bet that not 1 in 100 of them would have agreed that there was much to be gained by trying to make aircraft less detectable, particularly by radar. Some designers were enthusiasts for smaller, less expensive fighters, claiming that their smaller size would mean that they would be harder to detect, but that is not the same thing.

Every designer worth his salt knew the radar range equation, a relatively simple expression of physical fact. Detection range varied with the fourth root of radar cross-section (RCS), the standard measure of an object's reflectivity. Consequently, even if the RCS could be halved—which seemed unlikely in a discipline where a 10 percent improvement in any key performance number is a triumph—the result would be a not-very-useful one-sixth reduction in detection range. Designers natu-

rally concluded that RCS was an unrewarding area and spent little engineering effort on it.

Most designers felt the same way in 1975, unaware that a small group of people in the United States, divided into two industry teams and their government customers in the Pentagon, were working frantically to design and build aircraft that would blow the conventional wisdom out of the water. Halving the RCS was a goal that they had long left behind them. These new low-observables (LO) designs, also called stealth aircraft, would show RCS numbers 100 to 1,000 times smaller than any conventional fighter or bomber. They would convert almost any radar-controlled system in the world into junk, the massive Soviet air defense network included.

Stealth did not have a single inventor, nor did it have a neat chain of inventors, each one improving on the work of his predecessor. Rather, the work divided itself among many people with different gifts and talents. There were the Leonardos, the artist-theoreticians who envisioned what most people believed to be impossible. They leaped lightly over difficulties great and small, and it was the Edisons who solved them as they were discovered. "Inventing to schedule," it was called. The Medicis were a group of civilian and

The Rockwell B-1 was the only major combat aircraft of the pre-stealth era to be designed with a reduced radar cross-section as part of the requirement. Clearly visible in this head-on view of the later, production B-1B are the streamwise baffles added to the inlet ducts of the aircraft. These block the line-of-sight to the compressor faces of the GE F101 engines. *Rockwell*

The production version of the Horten HoIX would have been skinned with a radar-absorbing plywood sandwich material, one of many ways (including its internal layout) in which it foreshadowed the B-2. *Motor-Buch Verlag*

uniformed Pentagon leaders who knew when to apply pressure and when to provide support.

Until a few years ago, the identities of many of these people were secret. Only a few had been named in public. The names of others could be heard in quiet corners, found in the credits of obscure technical papers, or guessed at from a vague hint at "special programs" in a biography. Interview requests were formally declined or lost in a clearance system that would try the tolerance of Job himself. Northrop's Tacit Blue, second in significance among the early stealth prototypes, lay in a sealed hangar for a decade after its flying career ended. Its existence was as secret as that of the base where it was stored.

They were a small group and they remain close-knit, even with their former rivals. They are quicker to grant credit than to claim it. Their bonds were forged in months and years of intense collaboration and competition, of endless working binges under rigorous, paranoid secrecy. A professor of psychology, the spouse of one of the pioneers, compares them to people who have lived through a common trauma, like a battle or a natural disaster, that others have not experienced.

Like most inventions, stealth was an innovative use of the familiar rather than a bolt of wisdom from the blue. The first stealth systems were a natural

Small size—compared to a contemporary bomber—was expected in itself to make the U-2 less detectable. But the relationship of size to detectability was poorly understood, and Soviet radar tracked the aircraft successfully from the outset. *Lockheed*

One of the more extraordinary attempts to reduce RCS involved the installation of a perimeter of treated wires around a U-2. Kelly Johnson called it "the dirty bird." *Chris Pocock*

The wires were intended to create a precisely phased radar echo that would cancel the real echo from the skin. The experiment was abandoned after the Soviet Union sent the United States an accurate track of the "dirty bird's" route over its territory. *Chris Pocock*

response to the advent of radar, which had advanced from a technical gimmick to a crucial weapon by mid-1940. German technologists discovered that certain materials—carbon products in particular—absorbed radar waves rather than reflecting them. The process was little understood, and the methods of making and using this early radar-absorbent material (RAM) were empirical, but German industry did manage to develop RAM that could be applied to the snorkel tubes of the Navy's U-boats. In this application, RAM did not have to work very well in order to conceal a small target in a welter of random reflections (what radar designers called clutter) from the sea.

Two unconventional German aircraft designers, the brothers Walter and Reimar Horten, were the first engineers to propose the use of RAM on an aircraft. Like Jack Northrop in the United States, the Hortens were zealous advocates of flying-wing aircraft. By 1942, they were working on the Horten HoIX, a twin-jet flying-wing fighter-bomber, flying the prototype in 1944. To preserve strategic materials, the HoIX had a steel-tube frame covered with plywood skins. On the production aircraft, the Hortens proposed to use a sandwich skin material comprising two thin plywood sheets and a core of sawdust, adhesive, and carbon. The sole purpose of carbon was to absorb radar waves and make the aircraft less detectable by radar.

In the 10 years after the war, the development of RAM continued in the United States and the United Kingdom. The development followed several tracks. In the United Kingdom, a good deal of work was directed at using RAM on ship superstructures, although it was also tested on Canberra reconnaissance aircraft.

In late 1956, in the United States, work on what was then called "radar camouflage" took a more practical turn, under one of the nation's most secret programs.

In 1954, Lockheed's chief designer, the formidable Clarence L. "Kelly" Johnson, had formed a hand-picked team to develop a new spyplane for the Central Intelligence Agency (CIA). Johnson had made an unsolicited proposal to the CIA, which was already working with the USAF, Martin, and Bell on the same requirement. Johnson promised to deliver an aircraft with better range and altitude performance than his rivals, and do it faster and in total secrecy. Designed in Burbank, the aircraft were assembled in a nondescript, unmarked plant near Bakersfield. Test pilot Tony LeVier helped to find a secret test base: a remote airfield on the edge of the dry Groom Lake in Nevada, within the USAF's Nellis

Visible on these Lockheed A-12 supersonic spyplanes, under construction at Burbank, are the "pie-slice" fiberglass/plastic inserts placed in the wing leading edges to reduce RCS. The inward slope of the vertical tails was also an RCS-reduction measure. *Lockheed*

training and weapons range and just to the east of the Atomic Energy Commission's nuclear test site. The AEC divided the land around the test site into numbered areas for fallout tracking and other purposes. The secret flight test base was in Area 51.

Ten years earlier, Johnson had formed a small, selective, multidisciplinary team to build the XP-80 jet fighter. The team's partitioned-off prototype shop reminded Lockheed people of the secret moonshine factory in the comic strip *Li'l Abner*—the "Skonk Works." The spelling was changed but

the name stuck—to Johnson's undying distaste. Formally, Johnson's team became known as the Advanced Development Projects (ADP) division of Lockheed-California.

The CIA's new spyplane, the U-2, made its first flight from Area 51 in August 1955, eight months after metal was cut, and made its first overflight of the Soviet Union in July 1956.

From the outset, neither Johnson nor the CIA's project director, Richard Bissell, believed that the U-2 could defy the Soviet air defenses

Radar-absorbent edges are visible on this A-12 and on the D-21 supersonic reconnaissance drone carried on its back. The D-21 was among the lowest-RCS vehicles of the 1960s. *Lockheed*

with impunity for more than two years, but they were surprised when the first flights were tracked and fighters were launched in an attempt to shoot the U-2s down. This was a disappointment for President Dwight Eisenhower, who did not want to provoke the Russian leadership and who had been told by the CIA that the Soviet defenses would probably overlook a single, small U-2.

Consequently, only a few months after the first mission, Lockheed started a project to reduce the U-2's detectability by radar—primarily,

by long-range, low-frequency early-warning radars working in the 65–85 megahertz (MHz) range. Two approaches were tested. Under Project Rainbow, a prototype U-2 was fitted with an elaborate system of thin-gauge wires, supported by nonconductive poles (first bamboo and later fiberglass) around the wing and tail, and stretching to the nose and fuselage. The wire formed a perimeter, standing off from the leading and trailing edge of the wing by about a foot. The wire carried precisely spaced ferrite beads. The Rainbow system, also known as the trapeze,

North American, with stealth experience on the Hound Dog missile, proposed applying RCS-reduction measures to the XB-70 Valkyrie Mach 3 strategic bomber. Such a venture might have seemed equivalent to hiding an elephant in a strawberry patch by painting its toenails red, but some features of the XB-70—such as serpentine inlet ducts and highly swept, sharp leading edges—would have made it possible to reduce nose-on RCS. *Rockwell*

was designed to create a radar echo that would mimic the echo from the airframe—but half a wavelength out of phase, so that it would precisely null the natural echo. The second approach was nicknamed "wallpaper." A flexible plastic material containing a layer of printed circuits, it was glued to parts of the U-2's fuselage, nose, and tail.

In May 1957, Richard Bissell told Eisenhower that the "majority of incidents [U-2 overflights] would be undetected" once the Rainbow and "wallpaper" modifications were implemented. His confidence was utterly misplaced. The Rainbow modifications were "not very successful," in the words of the CIA's official history, and lopped 1,500 feet off the U-2's cruising altitude. The "wallpaper" modification acted as an insulator. On April 2, 1957, a modified U-2 (in fact, the first prototype) was lost when

One of the earliest systematic approaches to RCS reduction was carried out by Ryan Aeronautical Company (Teledyne Ryan after 1969), which embarked in 1962 on a secret program to develop reconnaissance versions of the Firebee target drone. This early example has RAM blankets on its side and a mesh screen over the inlet. *Teledyne Ryan*

its engine flamed out due to overheating. Test pilot Robert Sieker was killed. Johnson gave the modified aircraft the uncomplimentary nickname "dirty birds."

Nevertheless, testing continued. At first, the modified U-2s were flown over an experimental radar site on the ground. This was a cumbersome procedure, because each overflight covered only a small range of viewing angles. The Skunk Works devised a scheme in which a complete aircraft could be hoisted on to a 50-foot pylon, allowing the airplane's radar reflectivity to be tested on the ground.

A total of nine "dirty bird" flights crossed the Soviet Union, most of them in late 1957. In March 1958, a radar-camouflaged U-2 overflew the Soviet Far East. The Soviet Union protested vigorously—and, moreover, presented the United States with an aide-memoire that described the U-2's track in great detail. This told the CIA that Soviet radar operators had experienced no trouble in tracking the camouflaged aircraft, and the use of the Rainbow and wallpaper modifications was discontinued.

The abandonment of the radar-camouflaged U-2 lent more urgency to the CIA's search for a replacement. Lockheed had started studies of a supersonic replacement for the U-2 in 1957. Also, the company was working on the Air Force–sponsored, hydrogen-fueled CL-400 Suntan project. The CIA, meanwhile, approached Convair—which was developing the Air Force's B-58 supersonic bomber—and persuaded the company to take an interest in a future spyplane.

In September 1958, a committee chaired by Edwin Land (the inventor of the Polaroid camera) reviewed a range of potential U-2 replacements. The committee rejected the CL-400 (which was finally canceled in February 1959). Johnson offered two other designs. One

Further RCS reductions were incorporated into the Ryan reconnaissance drones as more specialized, long-range and high-altitude versions were developed. The Model 147T used North American's RCS-reduction technology. *Teledyne Ryan*

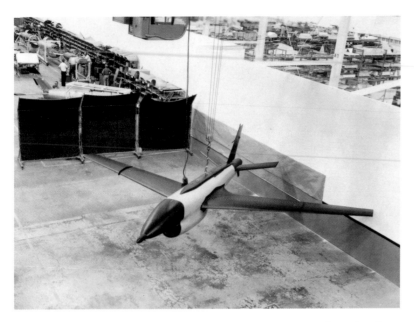

After the Lockheed U-2 and A-12, Ryan's drones were the first aircraft to undergo full-scale radar cross-section testing, on a range built by Teledyne Micronetics. This is the full-scale RCS model of the Model 147T. *Teledyne Ryan*

RCS, with ceramic wing leading edges and fiberglass inlet ducts leading to buried engines.

Some of the CIA representatives on the selection team favored the low-RCS Convair design. Lockheed, however, had a better record of delivering aircraft on time and on cost, and had a strong working relationship with the CIA in terms of security. The selection panel awarded the development contract to Lockheed at the end of August, but required Lockheed to demonstrate that the A-12's RCS could be reduced.

Before winning the contract to build the A-12, Johnson's team had started work on a full-scale model of the aircraft, built specifically to be mounted on a pylon for RCS testing. Edgerton, Germeshausen & Grier (EG&G), a technology-services company founded by Massachusetts Institute of Technology (MIT) faculty members, built a new RCS testing range—probably at Area 51—for the program.

Tests continued into early 1960, resulting in significant changes to the A-12's shape. In particular, the engineers realized that the rounded body and

was a new supersonic design, called the Archangel-2 or A-2 (the name derived from the U-2's early nickname at Lockheed, the "Angel"), powered by turbojets and ramjets. The other was a subsonic tailless flying wing, code-named Gusto 2A, with a strong emphasis on low RCS. Neither was accepted, and the committee showed more interest in Convair's Fish, a small ramjet-powered aircraft designed to be launched from a stretched, more powerful B-58.

Early in 1959, the CIA focused on two potential solutions, a refined runway-take-off design from Lockheed and Convair's air-launched system. Moreover, the CIA had been persuaded by theoretical research that an aircraft with reduced radar cross-section, flying fast and high, could evade radar detection. The "blip-scan" theory held that a weak echo, changing position rapidly between scans, would be rejected as noise.

Both companies submitted designs in the summer of 1959. Lockheed's A-11 was a Mach 3.2 airplane and was not heavily influenced by reduced RCS. Convair's smaller, air-launched Fish was a Mach 4.2 lifting-body design that made extensive use of pyroceramic materials, which could resist heat but could be treated to absorb radar signals. Both designs were rejected, Lockheed's because it did not meet the RCS requirement and Convair's because it was risky; also, the USAF, in June, had canceled the B-58B Super Hustler that was supposed to carry it.

Both teams were told to start again. By late summer, Lockheed had modified the A-11 into the A-12, with a reduced RCS. Convair produced a completely new design, the Kingfish, which took off from a runway with turbojet engines. However, the design still emphasized low

Ultimate stealth aircraft of the 1960s was Teledyne Ryan's AQM-91A Firefly, developed under the air force's Compass Arrow program. It appears that the Firefly under the left wing of the DC-130 launch and control aircraft has lost some of its RAM paint during tests. *Teledyne Ryan*

The Firefly's engine was mounted above the body, shielding the inlet from radar and reducing the infrared detectability of the exhaust. The twin vertical fins were canted inward. The normal recovery technique was for the vehicle to descend by parachute and be recovered in flight by helicopter. *Teledyne Ryan*

nacelle sides created a strong radar reflection at any angle. From the RCS viewpoint, it was better to flare the body smoothly outward to a sharp edge, resulting in the characteristic "chined" shape of the A-12's forebody. Also, the structure was redesigned to incorporate RAM. Since there was no material available that would act as RAM and still carry the structural and thermal loads imposed on the airframe, the Lockheed designers devised a saw-toothed structural configuration for the chines and wing leading edges. The "teeth" were triangular titanium structures that gave the edges strength. The gaps between the teeth were filled with a radar-absorbent honeycomb plastic material, skinned with a heat-resistant fiberglass.

From the side, the largest spike in the remaining radar signature was caused by the vertical stabilizers. The Lockheed team accordingly canted the stabilizers 15 degrees inward and even made them out of nonmetallic materials—in 1960, an immense leap in the state of the art. The production aircraft would be painted with a RAM coating comprising ferrite particles in a plastic binder.

The combined RCS-reducing measures were successful as far as they went. However, some areas could not be addressed. For example, the head-on RCS remained dominated by the inlet lips, which could not be RAM-treated or canted.

Ultimately, the low-RCS technology on the A-12 proved less useful than expected. By 1962, U.S. intelligence had detected the Soviet Union's massive P-14 early-warning radar, code-named Tall King, and its computer-based control and display system. The P-14's performance undermined the blip-scan theory. The level of RCS reduction achieved on the A-12 would not prevent an adversary from detecting it. In the U.S. Air Force's variants of the A-12—the YF-12A experimental interceptor and the SR-71 Black-bird strategic reconnaissance aircraft—the chines and vertical tails reverted to metal. The Blackbirds survived through speed and altitude.

Nevertheless, the stealth technology used on the A-12 remained classi-fied—to the point that technical papers on the Blackbird design contained deliberately misleading explanations for features such as the chines and the canted fins. More than a decade after the A-12's fighter variant, the YF-12, was unveiled, Northrop's stealth guru, John Cashen, was utterly astonished to hear Kelly Johnson describe its RCS-reducing features at a secret symposium at

Lockheed ventured into a specialized area of LO in the late 1960s, modifying Schweizer sailplanes into ultraquiet reconnaissance aircraft with muffled engines and multiblade propellers. The U.S. Army planned to use them to reconnoiter trails in Vietnam. This is the aft-engined Q-Star. *Lockheed*

Wright-Patterson Air Force Base. "Nobody had figured out that the SR had stealth," Cashen recalls. "I sat there with my mouth open."

Apparently, Lockheed's work on RCS reduction was placed on the back burner after the A-12 was developed. However, Lockheed was not the only company working in this area.

In August 1957, North American had won a contract to develop a jet-powered supersonic stand-off missile, the GAM-77 (later AGM-28) Hound Dog, to arm the B-52G bomber. The Hound Dog was designed to destroy missile and radar sites in the bomber's path. The first production missiles were delivered late in 1959, but it was soon realized that the weapon itself was easy to detect and shoot down. The program was on the point of being canceled, but North American developed a set of RAM components and coatings—many of them applied to the engine inlet—which reduced the missile's nose-on RCS and shifted the balance against the defender. Modified missiles were delivered from 1962 onward, and the weapon remained in service until 1975. The sensitive technology was referred to as "highly integrated defensive electronics" (HIDE).

The Hound Dog low-RCS program was moved to Tulsa, Oklahoma, in the early 1960s, and Tulsa became North American's center for such work. The company even proposed applying RAM to its XB-70 Valkyrie bomber, to reduce the dominant RCS spikes from its massive inlets. As

North American continued to study advanced bombers during the 1960s, RAM and shaping became important elements of their designs.

Some of the most remarkable low-RCS work in the 1960s was carried out by Ryan Aeronautical Company in San Diego (known as Teledyne Ryan Aeronautical, or TRA, after 1968). Builders of the widely used Firebee jet target drone, Ryan proposed a camera-carrying reconnaissance drone, the Model 136 Red Wagon, to the USAF in 1960. The high-altitude drone was designed with the engine above the fuselage, inward-canted twin tails, and a flat underside to reduce its detectability. The Model 136 was rejected; but, in 1962, Ryan was authorized to produce a reconnaissance drone based on a modified Firebee airframe.

It was the first of a series of Firebee-derived drones, collectively nicknamed Lightning Bugs. They were used operationally over North Vietnam, launched from C-130s and recovered by helicopters that used a trapeze to seize their parachute lines in flight. The earliest Lightning Bugs used wire-mesh screens over the inlets and RAM blankets on their body sides to reduce RCS. Later variants used North American's HIDE technology.

After several Firebees were shot down over China, the USAF finally showed interest in an all-new reconnaissance drone with low-RCS features built into its design. After a competition with North American, Ryan won a contract to develop a totally new high-altitude, long-range drone. The Model 154, or AQM-91 Firefly, was developed in great secrecy and made its first flight from Holloman AFB, New Mexico, in June 1968. It made its public debut in August 1969, when the fourth aircraft malfunctioned and descended by parachute into the Atomic Energy Commission's laboratory at Los Alamos—next to an employee picnic area and 100 yards from the fence.

The Firefly had a flat underside, angled body sides, and a top-mounted inlet and exhaust. The design showed evidence of serious attention to infrared signatures, with a specially designed exhaust mixer on its GE J97 engine. RAM was used not only as a surface treatment, but also as a structural material. Firefly was a sophisticated vehicle, with a highly accurate navigation system, and tests took some time. It was late 1971 before two test flights were performed against simulated Soviet SAM radars at China Lake, California. Tests showed that operators using the Fan Song B and E radars—which guided the SA-2 missile, widely used in China—had great difficulty tracking the drone unless they were given very accurate information about its position.

Unfortunately for the Firefly, Secretary of State Henry Kissinger beat it to China. With the Kissinger-Nixon diplomatic moves toward China in 1971, U.S. intelligence agencies were forbidden to launch drones over the country's military installations. The survivors of 28 Model 154s were retired to Davis-Monthan AFB on "ready-alert" status, and they later vanished.

Alongside the development of some experimental and operational low-RCS aircraft, the 1960s also saw more investment in test facilities. General Dynamics' research into RCS reduction did not end with the loss of the CIA contest to Lockheed's A-12 in 1959. Studies of Kingfish derivatives

The Rockwell B-1 was designed in 1970 to meet a target RCS figure. It was not designed to survive by stealth alone, but lower RCS would mean that its electronic jamming systems would need less power. Visible on this unpainted aircraft are RAM paint patches around antennas and the nose ride-control vanes, suppressing corner reflections. *Rockwell*

continued, and GD not only built its own RCS range but also built a new range for the USAF at Holloman AFB, operated by the USAF's RATSCAT (Radar Target Scatter) division. Other RCS work did not involve air vehicles. The developers of reentry vehicles (RVs) for intercontinental missiles were interested in the RCS characteristics of RVs, in order to counter or spoof potential defenses. McDonnell Douglas' missile division at Huntington Beach built an RCS range at Grey Butte, in the Mojave Desert, for RV work.

But this work on RCS reduction had almost no impact beyond a few specialized programs. One researcher recalls talking to fighter manufacturers about RCS reduction: "The problem was keeping them awake during briefings. The bottom line was that it cost them less to miss the RCS specification than to meet it."

The problem was that even the best that the designers could do was of limited use. The technology incorporated in the Model 154, which went further in RCS reduction than any other aircraft of the day, could reduce the defender's warning time but not allow the aircraft to complete its mission undetected. Even elaborate RCS-reduction measures worked only across a limited bandwidth and a certain set of aspect angles. Once hostile early-warning radar detected the aircraft, and tracking radars were cued on to it, the value of RCS reduction was almost zero.

Underlying this problem was a simple fact. The technology of the 1960s, including radar cross-section ranges, RAM and shaping, was not up to the job. Moreover, nobody knew what was needed to make RCS-reduction work; nobody knew where to look for a breakthrough; and nobody expected such a breakthrough to occur. But, within a few years, that is exactly what happened.

Chapter 2

HAVE BLUE AND THE ADVENT OF STEALTH

In the fall of 1974, the Pentagon's scientific consulting group, the Defense Science Board, completed its annual Summer Study. It was grim reading. The study looked at the likely outcome of an air war in Central Europe, and was heavily influenced by experience from the Yom Kippur war in the Middle East, in which the Israeli Air Force—using the latest U.S. equipment—had lost 100 aircraft in the first 18 days of operations, most of them to radar-guided SAMs. In some areas, the tide turned only when the Arab forces ran out of missiles.

The DSB concluded that U.S. aircraft would "have a real challenge getting through air defenses," recalls Allen Atkins, then a civilian mathematician at Wright-Patterson AFB. In fact, it projected that NATO air forces would lose aircraft so rapidly that they could not sustain operations.

Atkins recalls the genesis of today's stealth technology in the late summer and early fall of 1974. It emerged, he says, from two unrelated developments. After the successful use of remotely piloted vehicles (RPVs) in Vietnam, USAF and industry researchers were looking at smaller, less complex mini-RPVs and what they could accomplish in tactical missions.

In the process, a mini-RPV had been flown against both U.S. and foreign radars at Eglin AFB, and had proved very difficult to detect.

Atkins was working with a group at Wright-Patterson that supported the Defense Advanced Research Projects Agency (DARPA). It was in September or October, Atkins said, that the Pentagon's deputy director for research and engineering, Malcolm Currie, asked this group whether it would be possible to build a manned aircraft with a signature as low as the tiny mini-RPV. "We said we'd give it a try," says Atkins.

There were a number of basic obstacles to achieving lower RCS numbers. The first is what was known as the "fourth-root problem." Radar cross-section is a simple measure of the target's radar reflectivity. However, it is only one of a number of factors in the equation that determines the range at which a radar is likely to detect the target. Others include the power of the radar, the size of the antenna, and the radar's signal-to-noise ratio. Because of the geometry involved, detection range varies with the fourth root of RCS. What this means is that it takes a huge reduction in RCS to make a tactically significant difference in detection range.

Lockheed's Have Blue design was initially tested in the form of a small RCS model, in an indoor RCS test range. At that time, large indoor RCS ranges did not exist. The pyramidal shapes lining the walls are made from carbon-loaded plastic foam, which absorbs radar. *Lockheed*

Suppose that a radar can detect a target with a 10-square-meter RC at 100 miles. Halve the RCS, and the detection range is still 85 miles. Even at a 1-square-meter RCS, detection range is cut by less than half—a difference that a good radar engineer could quickly make up. To make a real difference and open up large gaps in a chain of radars, the aircraft designer needs to reduce RCS by a factor of 100 to 1,000. Nobody, in 1970, had any idea how this could be done.

Even if a very low RCS could be achieved, there was no way to confirm that it had been done. The existing RCS ranges such as Grey Butte and RATSCAT were not "quiet" enough to measure a very small target.

Northrop's proposed Have Blue design had a diamond-shaped planform and an over-the-body inlet. It was the former feature that proved a decisive disadvantage, because Northrop could not go to the extreme sweep angles found on the Lockheed aircraft. *Northrop*

Below

This is an early version of the Have Blue design. As finally built, the aircraft had more acute sweep on the trailing edges of the wing, to reduce detectability from the rear. *Lockheed*

An early Have Blue model mounted on a "pole," or pylon, for RCS testing. The first RCS range pylons were simple vertical beams wrapped in foam-plastic RAM, but it was soon discovered that they reflected too much energy to test very stealthy shapes. *Lockheed*

Late in 1974, DARPA contacted the main U.S. manufacturers of fighters and other military aircraft, to determine which of them might be interested in bidding on the study. At some point, it acquired the nickname "Harvey," an ironic reference to the 6-foot invisible rabbit that haunted James Stewart in the movie of the same name. Several of the key participants have referred to it by that name, although others have said that the name was never used.

The term "stealth" had been used in the context of manned aircraft as far back as 1966, by C. E. "Chuck" Myers, a combat pilot and Lockheed executive who was one of the founders of the so-called "fighter Mafia." Myers was an advocate of smaller, lighter fighters than the USAF was planning at the time, and pushed their smaller visual and radar signatures as tactical advantages.

Later, working at the Pentagon, Myers became an advocate for extremely small fighter aircraft. One inspiration was Britain's Folland Gnat, a tiny fighter with a 5,000-pound-thrust engine, which had been used effectively by the Indian Air Force in its air battles with Pakistan. By the early 1970s, Myers was promoting a concept for a "microfighter." He expected it to be stealthy, as a byproduct of its small size. By 1974–1975, the name was applied to the LO project.

Reflections from the ground and noise in their instrumentation systems would simply drown a small echo.

Another problem: USAF researchers did not believe that the low numbers were attainable. Working in the USAF's Radar Test Building, a unique all-wooden building (constructed with wooden pegs instead of nails) on the fringe of the Wright-Patterson AFB campus, the USAF's Bill Bahret had come to be regarded as "the father of radar camouflage" for his pioneering work on signatures in the 1950s. Atkins recalls that Bahret "had driven a stake into the ground. He had said that for a given size and volume, you'd never get below a certain level of RCS."

But the most serious challenge was fundamental. There was no accurate way to tell how well a certain combination of shape and materials would work in terms of reducing RCS, short of a large-scale physical experiment. In 1991, Dr. Vaughn Cable, then the leader of the Skunk Works signatures group, described the engineering methods that were used in the 1950s and 1960s. "Models were built—in partial and full-scale—tested, modified, put back on the pole and retested, many, many times. And, as you can imagine, there's a pretty lengthy wall-clock time associated with this iterative process of design. Only a limited number of cases could be dealt with before a typical program would run out of money." It was rather like trying to design an airplane without any mathematical aerodynamic theories or a wind-tunnel.

There was still some interest in RCS reduction. North American Rockwell's B-1 design clearly reflected some attention to RCS. Teledyne Ryan worked with USAF researchers on a delta-shaped low-RCS design, and was even awarded a patent in 1975. McDonnell Douglas studied a "quiet" attack aircraft for the U.S. Navy, producing a design that bore an eerie resemblance to the company's first fighter, the XP-67 of World War II. But the goal of an RCS so low that it would reliably delay detection seemed beyond reach.

A later, near-definitive Have Blue model on the "pole" at the Air Force's RATSCAT range, located at Holloman Air Force Base in New Mexico. The pylon is the new design developed by Lockheed, sloped and with a sharp edge facing the radar. *Lockheed*

The first Have Blue article had a short career and few images have been released. Intended to prove the design's flying qualities, it had no RAM coating and was equipped with a spin-recovery parachute. The camouflage scheme was designed to mask its shape from observers. *Lockheed*

Stealth had a low profile at first, and was not particularly secret, because nobody knew whether or not it would even be important. The project formally started in January 1975, with small contracts to McDonnell Douglas and Northrop, but not Lockheed, calling for designs for a low-RCS manned aircraft. Neither weapons nor sensors need be carried and at this stage there was no guarantee that there would be money to take the project further. "For some reason," Atkins recalls,

"the DARPA office touched base with only one division at Lockheed, and they didn't indicate that they wanted to bid."

Since the project was not highly classified, it was not surprising that it came to the attention of Ben Rich, who took over control of the Skunk Works in January 1975. By the time Rich heard of it, however, DARPA had spent all of the project funds, so the Skunk Works worked under a no-cost contract.

Rich asked Warren Gilmour, the Skunk Works' head of operational research, to put together a Harvey team. Gilmour called Denys Overholser, who was laid up at home after making an ill-advised use of his leg as a toboggan brake. Overholser was younger than many of the Skunk Works designers—unlike many others, including Harvey program manager Dick Scherrer, he had joined after the incredibly difficult Blackbird program. He was also an electrical engineer and mathematician by training, in a business where aerodynamicists ruled the roost. Overholser's specialty at the Skunk Works was radomes and antennas.

Overholser was back on his feet and back at work in May. "I went to see Dick Scherrer," he recalls, "and told him how to make an airplane invisible."

"You needed the mathematics," Overholser says, "but you need to have a feeling for the solution as well. Otherwise you can write a computer program and still not know if the computer is giving you the right answer. The computer gives you the answer to two decimal places."

The second Have Blue, probably before its first flight. Covers protect its inlets and RAM-treated wing leading edges. To speed assembly, the aircraft used many existing parts, including a T-38 landing gear. *Lockheed*

Faceting on Have Blue was simpler than it was on the later F-117. Also, the landing gear doors and canopy edges do not feature the serrations used on the later aircraft. *Lockheed*

Overholser knew his RCS. "A flat panel," he points out, "is the brightest target, and also the dimmest." If the panel is at right angles to the incoming beam, it is an enormous target. Rotate it in one dimension, however, and most of the energy is deflected away from the radar. Rotate it in two directions and the panel's RCS becomes infinitesimal. So, reasoned Overholser, make an airplane entirely out of flat panels, angled so that none is ever likely to be normal to a radar.

Gilmour recognized the logic in the approach. He was aware that, in Vietnam, snipers had detected U.S. Army helicopters by sun glints from their curved windows. (Lockheed-California had made a foray into attack helicopters in the 1960s.) When they were replaced by flat panels, the helicopters were less visible.

One of the first steps was to build a model of the strange diamond-shaped airplane that resulted from applying Overholser's principles. Its RCS was too small to be measured at Lockheed's facilities. "They decided that I wasn't the village idiot, so I became a genius instead," says Overholser. Veteran designer Dick Cantrell, however,

decided that it was an aerodynamic disaster and nicknamed it the Hopeless Diamond.

From the customer's viewpoint, it was clear that Lockheed and Northrop had outdone their competition. "They were very aggressive," Atkins recalls. "They threw the paradigm away and looked at the problem in a different manner." During the summer of 1975, Ken Perko of DARPA and the USAF's Bill Elsner worked on a plan to build and test a prototype stealth aircraft.

In September, the two companies were asked to propose a test program. Each would design a small prototype aircraft, to prove that a real stealth aircraft would fly and that it could evade radar. At the same time, the companies would build full-scale models for a "pole-off" at the USAF's RCS range at Holloman AFB. The design that performed better on the pole would be chosen for flight test. The companies were given two months to prepare their proposals and five months to carry them out. The project's name changed from Harvey to the more respectable Experimental Survivable Testbed, or XST.

Have Blue was a radically simple stealth design, with a sharper leading-edge sweep than the F-117. It had large one-piece elevons for pitch and roll control. Handling qualities were marginal, leading to the significant aerodynamic differences in the later F-117. *Lockheed*

The fight was on. The teams joined forces to improve the USAF's RCS range so that the new designs could be tested, but otherwise the competition was fierce. "We were all working 12 to 16 hours a day, seven days a week," says Northrop's Irv Waaland. The engineers traveled from their Southern California offices to the McDonnell Douglas RCS range at Gray Butte in the Santa Susana mountains, or to Holloman. (Although McDonnell Douglas' XST design had been eliminated early in the program, the Gray Butte range was considered the best in the country, with excellent performance and low noise.) At the USAF's RCS range, the teams shared a hangar, divided by a black curtain. "We weren't supposed to peek, but it wouldn't have mattered," Waaland says. There was no time for major design changes.

Northrop had a problem. The Northrop XST had been designed on the assumption that the nose-on RCS was more important than the rear aspect. Its plan view shape was a lopsided diamond with more sweep on the leading edges than the trailing edges. From the rear, it sustained its low RCS

gram called Echo, which would provide a first-cut check on the RCS of the evolving design.

In August 1975, Alan Brown joined the Lockheed stealth team. Born and trained in the United Kingdom, Brown was a newcomer to the Skunk Works, having worked on a variety of projects, including Lockheed's supersonic transport design and missile warheads. "I was asked to come over for six weeks to help with the inlets and exhaust," Brown remarks. The six weeks turned into 16 years.

"We were surprisingly fortunate on the XST," Brown would say later. "It went better than we deserved." Lockheed had designed a notched trailing-edge for its XST, rather than a diamond shape. This had allowed the team to sharpen the sweep angles on the rear of the aircraft and meet the DARPA rear-quadrant requirement. Brown says that Lockheed's designers "went overboard" on some of the details of the design. Although Overholser had adapted the work of a Russian scientist, Pyotr Ufimtsev, in dealing with edges and the junctions between the flat panels, the junctions were all arranged to face the less critical side quadrants. "We avoided what we did not understand," says Brown. Ufimtsev's work was important, but not as vital as some sources have suggested.

Brown's own experience proved useful. Overholser's design philosophy forbade curves, even on the top or bottom of the wing, because they could not be modeled or predicted. The XST's hexagonal wing section appalled conventional aerodynamicists. But in Britain, Brown had worked on the Bloodhound surface-to-air missile, which had a similar wing section. His studies showed that a wing as sharply swept as that of the XST, with a sharp leading edge, "really flies on the vortex generated from the leading edge, and conventional two-dimensional aerodynamics really don't apply at all." Inside one of Lockheed's cavernous hangars, engineers tossed XST free-flight models from the fourth-floor mezzanine to check their flight characteristics.

Aerodynamicist Cantrell was still unconvinced. When a colleague asked him whether ice might form behind the facet edges, Cantrell commented that any ice formation would only improve the airplane's aerodynamics.

Alan Brown was responsible for the XST's extraordinary engine inlets. The Blackbird had used RAM in the inlet ducts to absorb the radar energy bouncing off the engine, but that approach would not yield RCS levels to match the much lower signature of the XST. Brown blended electromagnetics and aerodynamics, creating a grid of knife-edged slats, sharply swept back in the vertical and horizontal planes. The slats were so close together that the grid seemed to a radar to be a solid surface. Like the wing, they were highly swept and generated strong vortices, stabilizing the airflow even at high pitch or sideslip angles. (Northrop's prototype would have had wire

as long as the radar was no more than 35 degrees off the tail, but beyond that, the radar would be at right angles to the trailing edge. Unfortunately, the DARPA requirement treated RCS by quadrants. The rear quadrant extended to 45 degrees on either side of the tail, taking in the Northrop design's RCS spikes. Waaland could not solve the problem by stretching the tail and increasing the sweep angle, because the diamond-shaped aircraft would become uncontrollable.

Lockheed was inventing on a schedule, as the engineers called it. Before the proposal went in, Scherrer realized, according to Overholser, that Lockheed had to show the customer that its designers understood the shaping technique "and that the way to do that was to write a program." Overholser and his mentor, Bill Schroeder, sat down to work on a program based on a standard 1950s formula for radar scattering. It worked by dividing the polygonal facets into triangles and computing the RCS of each triangle. They worked independently, cross-checking their calculations to avoid errors, and in five weeks had written a pro-

27

Have Blue catches the morning sun over Area 51. The patchy color and texture of the skin show where RAM panels have been attached and removed, and where gaps have been sealed with tapes and putties. *Lockheed*

mesh over the inlet, which would have worked for a prototype but not for a faster operational aircraft.)

Lockheed made full use of its RAM technology, having obtained the CIA's permission to brief DARPA on it. "DARPA didn't realize how good we were," says Overholser. Lockheed's XST would be completely covered with RAM that resembled floor tile, with fiberglass honeycomb RAM on its edges.

In March 1976, the leaders of the two teams went to the Pentagon to present the results of their RCS and wind-tunnel tests and their prototype proposals. In a secure room, Perko and Elsner listened to each team, assessed their results and made their decision on the spot, but it was not to be announced until the next day. Ken Perko invited the competitors to spend the evening at his house in Virginia's horse country—and it was barely surprising that, as Irv Waaland recalls, "you could cut the air with a knife." Waaland and Cashen were relatively unknown alongside Kelly Johnson and Ben Rich. Already, says Waaland, "we felt that we weren't going to win."

The decision was announced the next day. Northrop's airplane was expected to fly better, but Lockheed was more stealthy and that was the point of the exercise. Cashen commented later that "We'd done a good job, but I had an immature RAM capability. I could prove on the pole that I was as good as they were. They had won by a whisker, and if the rules had been different it might have gone differently. But they could turn their design into a real airplane and I had a long way to go."

Lockheed was awarded a contract to build two XST prototypes. The target date for the first flight was 20 months from April 1, 1976, the effective date of the contract.

The trick of stealth is in the details, Overholser says, and it was the details that accounted for the 100-hour weeks that became the routine. Inlets. Exhaust nozzles. Drain holes. Door seals. Shadows and multiple reflections. All of these could ruin the design's stealth qualities, "but the computer didn't give answers at all."

Two problems proved particularly difficult. Wind-tunnel tests had shown that the dart-shaped prototype would be unstable above 17 degrees angle of attack. No matter how smart the computer-aided fly-by-wire flight control system might be, the controls would simply not have the power to prevent the aircraft from swapping ends. The prototype would have buzzers and a stick-shaker to warn the pilot as the limit approached, and a flap behind the engine exhausts—nicknamed the platypus—which would automatically force the nose down if the pilot ignored the warnings. The other major problem was the exhaust itself. Designed as a narrow slit for good stealth qualities, its natural tendency was to attempt to become a cylinder under heat and pressure. Designer Henry Combs led the team that produced an acceptable exhaust structure.

Meanwhile, another change had come over the program. Alan Brown traces it to the first Lockheed and Northrop tests of one-third-scale models at the Gray Butte range, in the fall of 1975. The RCS numbers were far lower than anyone had dreamed of predicting a year earlier, low enough to render many radars useless. "People realized that we had a tiger by the tail," says Brown. The XST project, which had been briefly mentioned in *Aviation Week* earlier in the year, was upgraded from Unclassified to Top Secret.

When Lockheed won the prototype contract in April 1976, the project moved further into the secret world. Like Lockheed's CIA spyplanes, it became an unacknowledged Special Access program (SAP). A SAP is a Pentagon program that operates under special security rules. It does not report in the normal way to Pentagon oversight organizations or to Congress, and the program manager has wide discretion in setting security rules within the program. (For example, SAPs are more likely than normal Pentagon programs to require polygraph tests for new employees.) An "unacknowledged" SAP is a program whose very existence is one of its core secrets—that is, its military utility would be compromised if its existence was disclosed. These projects are colloquially known as "black programs."

After the stealth project was declared an unacknowledged SAP, only those with a clear need-to-know would be told that the project even existed. The airplane would fly from the USAF's secret flight-test base at Area 51. The compromised designation XST vanished, to be replaced by the comfortably meaningless code-name Have Blue. People who had been involved with XST but not with the Lockheed effort were led to assume that XST had been terminated. The project office—now supported 51 percent by the USAF and 49 percent by DARPA—moved from Washington to a secure suite of offices, or "vault," at Wright-Patterson. For administrative purposes, it became part of the Mini-RPV System Project Office.

In the view of the insiders, the number of people with the need to know was extremely small. "The secretary of the Air Force, the three-star in charge of USAF research and development, and one or two other generals," knew about Have Blue, says Atkins. "There were four full-time people and six part-time at Wright-Patterson, and three or four people at DARPA."

Even the commander of the USAF's Aeronautical Systems Division, Lieutenant General George Sylvester, did not know what the Have Blue project was doing. Although the project office was a few minutes' walk from Sylvester's desk, it nominally reported to him through the mini-RPV organization, and he was technically responsible for all USAF aircraft development programs. The day of reckoning came a few months before the first flight. Because Have Blue was a manned aircraft, USAF regulations called for the design to undergo a safety inspection by an independent review team, appointed by the commander of ASD. Sylvester "about came unglued" when he realized that a pair of manned prototypes had been built without his knowledge, Atkins recalls.

Looking back, insiders believe that the secrecy was very important to the success of Have Blue, at a number of levels. Clearly, Have Blue's strange shape would point directly to the roots of its stealth technology if it was revealed. But as Alan Brown observes, "The purpose of secrecy is not just to protect information, but also to deny an adversary the knowledge that a problem has been solved. In the 1970s, most people thought that RCS reduction was not worth doing, because of the fourth-root problem. Nobody's going to put resources into a problem that can't be solved within a generation." Had the United States indicated the levels of RCS that were being achieved, he believes, other countries would have pushed stealth much harder.

As it was, Overholser notes, investigations in the 1990s showed that the Soviet Union had nine design bureaus working on stealth technology, "but they had all started work in 1985, after the announcement that we were building the B-2."

But secrecy was not entirely directed against the potential enemy. Some years ago, in a conversation with the author, an industry executive compared the "black" world to Australia—an isolated area in which unique creations can evolve, without being gobbled up by larger, more established predators before they reach maturity. Like the submarine or the tank, stealth was a high-risk technology that threatened the established way of doing things. Atkins agrees that secrecy probably helped protect the program "if it had gone the way of many other projects."

Dr. Paul Kaminski joined the stealth effort in early 1977, as an Air Force assistant to President Carter's new deputy secretary of defense for research and engineering, Dr. William Perry. Secrecy, says Kaminski, "stopped the foreign-body-rejection problem. One advantage of secrecy," he adds, "is that it prevents the liability of leadership. In a commercial business, you rarely find a leader introducing a radical new product. Why take the risk of upsetting the situation? With secrecy, the barriers are down and a new idea can mature."

Secrecy also protected the program from well-meaning intervention. "It was very important," says Brown. "We started with an extremely small program office, and later it got bigger—to the general detriment of the program, with too many self-styled experts putting in their two bits' worth." Atkins recalls working on a similarly risky program in DARPA's "white" side, the X-Wing vertical take-off aircraft. "We were getting ready to fly when Challenger crashed," in 1986, he says. "NASA said that we could not have that happen again, and started heavily scrutinizing the flight control system. Instead of a half-dozen people at meetings, we had 50, 60, or 70 people, and

The uneven, wavy contours of the RAM-covered skin are very apparent in this view—one of the advantages of the Have Blue design approach was that it did not call for immense precision in assembly. *Lockheed*

everybody had one question to ask. DARPA had estimated the cost of the flight control system at $10 million and the contractor estimated $8–9 million. When it passed $52 million, we shut the program down."

The small DARPA/USAF management team worked close to the edge of Pentagon rules, using secrecy as a justification for avoiding onerous reporting and monitoring tasks. "We saw no need to be as smart as the contractor was," says Atkins, "and there was a huge trust factor involved."

The two aircraft being assembled in Lockheed's Burbank plant were small vehicles. Their sole purpose was to show that a practical aircraft could emulate the low RCS numbers seen on the pole models. The aircraft were made entirely of conventional materials and used many off-the-shelf components. The landing gear was from an F-5. The nonafterburning General Electric J85-GE-4A engines were taken from Navy stocks of engines for the T-2C trainer.

The flight control system was taken from the General Dynamics YF-16 fighter prototype. The fly-by-wire system provided artificial stability, adjusting the controls many times a second to correct excursions from the desired flightpath. There was no fundamental reason why a stealthy aircraft could not be built with conventional mechanically signaled controls. However, the Have Blue—in common with aircraft featuring sharply swept wings and no horizontal tail, such as Concorde or the General Dynamics B-58—would have had an unusually high trim drag count if it was a naturally stable, nose-heavy design. The YF-16 flight control computers were also designed so that they could be adjusted easily to fine-tune the fighter's handling.

The two prototypes had different roles. Have Blue No. 1 was intended simply to show that the airplane would fly safely. It did not carry any RAM and it had a conventional, nonstealthy nose probe to carry speed, sideslip, and angle-of-attack sensors. The second aircraft was covered with RAM.

Most of the skin was covered with RAM sheets, comprising carbonyl iron particles in a flexible polymer binder. The material resembled linoleum; it was cut to shape and secured to the aluminum skin with adhesive. The wing edges used a material resembling that developed for the A-12, comprising a carbon-loaded core under a fiberglass skin. In fact, the material used on the A-12 was more complex than that used on the Have Blue, with 6 rather than 13 layers. To save time in development, the team relied heavily on RAM in the form of adhesive tapes and puttylike materials, which would be installed before every flight.

The first aircraft sported a strange camouflage scheme of jagged light and dark elements, which would make it harder for anyone to make out details of its shape if it happened to be caught in the open by a reconnaissance satellite. The second aircraft was painted in a light gray color.

Lockheed and the USAF had every intention of reducing the airplane's visual signature as well as its radar image. Combat experience in Vietnam had confirmed that, even in the radar era, the pilot who saw his opponent first had a tactical advantage. The USAF had engaged Cornell Laboratories (later known as Calspan) to develop ways to improve camouflage. Cornell rediscovered the principle of "Yehudi lights." Because a target outlined against a sky is much less illuminated than its background, the best way to hide it is to light it up. A group of Cornell researchers had formed a company named Scipar in Buffalo, New York, and Lockheed engaged its services to produce a visual camouflage system for the Have Blue. The airplane would have been painted light gray on its upper surfaces, fading to white underneath. Additionally, it would have had multiple light sources on its underside, connected by fiber-optic lines to a central light source. Photo-electric sensors on the upper surface would measure the luminance of the sky and modulate the light level automatically. The system was to be tested after the radar tests were complete.

The first aircraft was completed in November 1977. Lockheed's machinists were on strike, threatening the company's ability to make the contract deadline, so managers completed the aircraft. At one point, lacking a steel component for the exhaust structure, they sliced up a filing cabinet to make a temporary substitute. After final assembly, the wings were removed and a C-5 transport carried the prototype to Groom Lake.

At this time, Area 51 was an even more remote test location than it is today. Published accounts of the U-2 program had referred to a secret base in Nevada, known as "the Ranch" or "Watertown," but its exact location had not been publicly identified. The base had not expanded greatly since the days of the A-12 program. Its facilities comprised four large hangars at the northern end of the flight line, occupied by the Air Force/CIA "Red Hat" squadron and its collection of "acquired" Soviet aircraft; a bank of Navy-surplus housing units; and, to the south, the line of four double hangars built for the A-12s.

The main threats to security at the base were spies, spacecraft, and casually curious aircrew. The SAP rules were designed to weed out spies. In particular, it was a rare participant in an SAP who had not worked under conventional secrecy rules for several years. But there was always a chance that a long-term agent—a mole—had been planted by the Soviet GRU military intelligence organization years before. Compartmentalization was enforced. Most buildings were windowless. When classified tests were being carried out, those who did not have a direct need to observe the test activities were confined to their offices or corralled in a single space, such as the cafeteria.

The North American Air Defense (NORAD) headquarters, deep in its bunker at Colorado Springs, tracked the smallest objects in space with obsessional care and had a good idea about which of them were Soviet spy satellites. (In 1981, there was a minor security flap when it was revealed that NORAD's deep-space surveillance system had been used to check the orbiting Space Shuttle for damage to its heat-resistant tiles—NORAD did not want anyone to know how sharp its eyes were.) NORAD supplied Area 51 with a schedule of satellite overflights, and the flight-test schedule was arranged accordingly. If a satellite popped up unexpectedly—as a result of an orbital plane-change maneuver on the other side of the earth, for example—or if an unidentified aircraft appeared on course to the base, the flight-test team could use its "scoot-and-hide" shelters. These were simple structures close to the runways and taxiways, which would conceal the aircraft from sight.

Nellis AFB regularly hosted the massive Red Flag exercises, simulating the air war in Central Europe. Red Flag was only the largest of a number of exercises that brought hundreds of U.S. military aircraft and dozens of allied aircraft to Nellis. Aircrews were told that any infringement of the closed airspace around Area 51—controlled by a tower that used the call sign Dreamland—would cause them to be immediately packed off back to their units, like a child who has misbehaved at summer camp.

Security compounded the isolation for the people who worked at the base. There was no regular air service to the base; Las Vegas was several hours away by car, and engineers from Lockheed and other contractors could find themselves sequestered at Area 51 for weeks on end.

Long hours, secrecy, and weeks spent at remote locations took their toll on family life. One engineer's grade-school children told classmates that their father worked for the CIA, because nothing else seemed to fit. Working weeks comprised four days at the office and two on the road. Groom Lake had no nonsecure phones that could be used for calls home—families had one phone number that could be used to pass a message to a person working at the secret base, but it was made clear that it was for emergency use only. (Later, F-117 flight-test director Bill Fox succeeded in getting an outside phone installed in the Lockheed office.) Black-project workers associated mostly with one another when they were off duty, but even social occasions were stilted: spouses were out of the picture and workers could not discuss secrets—which meant everything that happened at work—outside secure facilities.

Have Blue made its first flight on December 1, 1977, in the hands of Lockheed's Bill Park. To nobody's great surprise, it was nobody's idea of a high-performance aircraft. It would have had a thrust-to-weight ratio more like a business jet than a fighter, even without the complex inlet and exhaust system, which drained more thrust from the engines, but its short wingspan and highly swept leading edge were inefficient at low speeds. The FBW system could fix many of the handling quirks—compensating for directional instability above Mach 0.65, for example—but only up to a point, because eventually the elevons and rudders could not move far or fast enough to compensate. Pilots were aware that the handling characteristics had a "cliff" in that Have Blue felt normal, but the handling characteristics would deteriorate rapidly if the limits were exceeded.

The first aircraft made 36 flights, shared between Park and USAF pilot Major Ken Dyson. It crashed on its 37th flight on May 4, 1978, done in by a device that was intended to assure its safety. Alan Brown was in the Groom Lake tower as test pilot Bill Park prepared to land after a series of fly-bys to gauge the airplane's visual signature. During the intense flight-test program, nobody had fully appreciated that Park was landing the aircraft at ever steeper angles of attack and steadily lower speeds, or had given thought to what might happen if the platypus operated on landing. On this day, Park finally overstepped the 17-degree limit, a few feet above the ground, and the emergency nose-down flap activated, slamming the prototype into the runway. Park pulled the aircraft off the ground and, reflexively, retracted the landing gear—the Have Blue was sluggish at low speeds and Park had learned to pull up the gear as soon as possible. But this was the worst thing Park could have done; the impact had damaged one of the main gears, and it jammed in a half-retracted position.

The F-117 was one of the last Lockheed aircraft to be built with the aid of a full-scale wooden mockup—it has now been replaced by computer models. The mockup was used to ensure that parts would fit and that different systems would not interfere with one another. *Lockheed*

Park tried to shake the gear loose, but with fuel running low he was ordered to abandon the prototype. He sustained a concussion when he ejected and further injuries when he landed, still unconscious, and was dragged across the desert floor by his parachute; the injuries ended his flying career.

The Have Blue prototype descended to the desert floor in a falling-leaf maneuver. It was physically intact, but the USAF decided that it could not be repaired to fly again. But what could be done with the hulk, and the priceless secrets that could be discerned in its every line? An Air Force construction team dug a hole in the desert at Area 51, and the historic airplane is buried there to this day. Alan Brown is not entirely sure that anyone kept an accurate record of the site—"I think they built a road across it"—and Hell will assuredly freeze over before the USAF lets any aviation archaeologists roam free across the Ranch.

Dyson flew the second Have Blue on July 20, and performed 52 flights over the next year. After 10 flights to check out the aircraft and systems, Dyson started flying the Have Blue against radars. The tests included ground-based and airborne emitters; U.S. radars and special systems intended to gather detailed RCS data; and devices that spanned a wide range of the electromagnetic spectrum, including the long-wavelength VHF band used by Soviet early-warning radars.

On July 11, 1979, Dyson was flying the Have Blue against an F-15 Eagle's radar when a weld in the exhaust duct failed. Hot exhaust gas leaked into the engine compartment, causing a failure in one of the two hydraulic systems. Before Dyson could get close to Area 51, the heat disabled the second system. Dyson no longer had any control over the aircraft's trajectory, and ejected; Have Blue No. 2 crashed near the Tonopah Test Range (TTR) and was destroyed. A few TTR workers scrambled into vehicles and headed for the crash site, but thought better of it after the F-15 pilot buzzed them at zero feet.

It may sound paradoxical to describe a program as a success when both prototypes crashed, but it is true in this case. The accidents were only indirectly related to stealth. They indicated the need for better solutions to stability and control problems, and underlined the fact that the narrow slitlike exhausts would be a challenge to design and build, but those were problems that could be fixed. The tests showed that a faceted stealth aircraft, with its design driven by stealth, could be made to fly reasonably well.

There were also some important lessons learned from the design. Have Blue underlined the importance of attention to apertures in the airplane, from access panels to landing gear doors. As the aircraft flexed under g loadings, and as aerodynamic pressures changed over its wings and body, gaps tended to change in width. In the flight test program, RAM "butter" had to be applied and allowed to dry before every RCS flight test.

Some issues remained unresolved. Have Blue did not demonstrate an adequate low-observable air data system, and it did not fly into icing. The inlets looked like ice-cube trays and were expected to work the same way.

Most important, the Have Blue flights proved that the real airplane had the same basic radar signature as the RCS pole model. The pole model had shown the RCS characteristics that had been predicted by computer analysis of the design, and the computer analysis tools had been able to model a design's RCS in a reasonable amount of time. When RCS test results were different from predictions, the engineers could analyze the differences, pinpoint their causes, and provide solutions.

In short, Have Blue had transformed low-RCS design into an engineering discipline. From now on, designers could set a target for RCS, design their aircraft to meet it, and be confident that it would work "on the pole" and in the air.

Chapter 3

SHAPE, SHAPE, SHAPE, AND MATERIALS

Stealth is camouflage. It is quite sophisticated camouflage, and covers a very wide spectrum of electromagnetic radiation and other signatures, but it is camouflage all the same, and shares some basic principles with the camouflage developed by nature.

One principle is that effective camouflage is not the same as being invisible. Most natural camouflage works by giving the object special visual features that resemble the prominent visual features of the background. A tiger is a very conspicuous object, but its largely vertical stripes have the same "signature" in terms of contrast, pattern and motion as the grass in which the tiger hides. In the Antarctic summer, a penguin resembles the bright whites and harsh shadows of the landscape. Against the sky above Vietnam, an F-4 painted in three-color olive/tan/earth stripes looks like an F-4 painted in three-color olive/tan/earth stripes. (Nobody said that human imitations of natural camouflage are always perfect.)

Radar camouflage, for an airplane, is a little different, in that the physical background is almost a blank. However, there is always noise in a radar system, produced by outside interference or internal electronics. This noise presents itself to the operator or the display processor as a blip, as a target does, and noise becomes the background against which the target conceals itself.

Another principle is that camouflage does not always have to defeat detection in order to work properly. For an attack to succeed, detection on its own is insufficient. The target must be detected in time, and then identified and tracked so that the attacker can plan a pursuit and endgame. Some zoologists have suggested that a zebra's stripes are not only aimed at concealment. Faced with the heaving sea of stripes in a herd of zebra, a predator cannot pick out or track a target. This principle was also exploited in the vivid "dazzle" camouflage schemes used on ships in World War I. The goal was not to conceal the ship, but to make it difficult for the observer—typically a U-boat captain, hanging on to a wobbly and salt-splashed periscope—to identify the class of the ship or indeed tell which end is which.

Likewise, a camouflaged attacker does not need to remain concealed throughout the attack. If I do not see the tiger until it is 20 feet away, I am in trouble. Likewise, a military aircraft is stealthy enough if it can close to within the range of its own weapons without being detected. For an

RCS testing was carried out at night, to avoid observation by spacecraft. *Lockheed*

An early lesson of stealth research was that skimping on the pole model was a false economy. The more accurate and detailed the model, the better the results. *Lockheed*

attacker, stealth is most important when it allows the attacker to approach the target, which usually means that frontal-sector stealth is most crucial.

In natural systems, camouflage is balanced across different spectra. An owl is visually camouflaged against predators, but its feathers and wing shape are not like those of birds that hunt mainly in the daytime. As a result, it is quieter in flight and even sharp-eared night animals are taken by surprise.

Such "balanced stealth" is a central concept in the design of low-observable aircraft. The objective is to reduce detection in every relevant spectrum to a proportionate level, so that there is no single dominant signature that betrays the target's presence long before other signatures are detected. In the case of the A-12, for example, the inlet lips were dominant in the nose-on radar signature. The designers could treat the airplane's body and wing edges with their revolutionary RAM structures, but hostile radars would still see the inlet lips. Modifying a conventional fighter to reduce its RCS is only effective to the point where the hostile radar sees its external fuel tanks and missiles. Beyond that point, any reduction in the RCS of the bare airframe is a waste of effort.

Balanced stealth extends beyond the radio-frequency spectrum. If an airplane cannot be detected by radar at a certain range, but can be readily picked up by an infrared sensor, its RCS is smaller than it needs to be. Skunk Works leader Ben Rich would stress that a stealth aircraft had to be stealthy in six disciplines: "Radar, infrared, acoustic, visual, smoke, and contrails—if you can't do that, you flunk the course."

If so, why does so much discussion of stealth focus on radar?

The answer is that radar is by far the most powerful means of detecting and tracking an airborne target and the linchpin of every air defense system in the world. No other sensor can detect an aircraft hundreds of miles away, regardless of weather; pin down its range, bearing, and altitude with great precision and little ambiguity; and determine its speed and course. Radar was a decisive factor in the Battle of Britain, not so much because Britain had superior radar technology (the hardware in the Chain Home system was crude) but because it had integrated radar into its fighter control system.

We talk about "seeing" targets on radar, but the analogy between sight and radar is weak. The daylight world is saturated with visible light that is

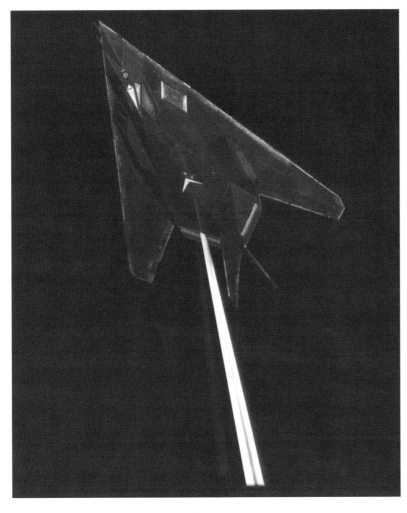

a sphere, with a cross-sectional area of one square meter. RCS can be expressed either as a number in square meters or in decibels (dB) relative to a square meter.

Lacking any basic, practical rules or laws that would allow them to control RCS, aircraft designers mostly ignored it. In the process, they made life very easy for the radar designers, because there are certain shape features that guarantee an enormous RCS. A flat plate, side-on to the radar beam, reflects energy very efficiently. Even worse is a right-angle corner. Like a double-bank shot on a pool table, it reflects energy straight back toward the radar at any angle. An open duct with a flat, reflective inner end is the worst of all. The energy bounces from side to side and off the inner end, and "comes romping out like a lighthouse beam" according to Lockheed's Alan Brown. Most jet inlets form such shapes, and they dominate the frontal RCS of nonstealthy aircraft.

A large jet aircraft such as a KC-135 has a frontal RCS of 100 square meters—like a semitrailer truck in side-view—and can be detected by any halfway decent radar at 200 miles range. An F-15 has a van-sized head-on RCS of 12 square meters, most of that being generated by the inlets.

These massive figures help explain why stealth works. Alan Brown compares the early mathematical RCS models to the aerodynamic theories that allowed early aviation pioneers to design airfoil sections. "It's like going from a brick to an airfoil," he has remarked. The early RCS codes were rudimentary, but they were an immense advance over the results of ignorance.

The principle of RCS reduction, as first applied to Have Blue, is actually very simple. A flat surface has an extremely large RCS if it is normal to the radar beam. As the plate is tilted or canted away from the beam in one dimension, its RCS decreases sharply: reflectivity is reduced by a factor of 1,000 (30 decibels) at a cant angle of 30 degrees. But if the same surface is rotated away from the beam on a diagonal axis—that is to say, it is both canted and swept back—the RCS reduction is much greater, so that a 30-decibel reduction can be realized at an 8 degree angle.

When Overholser told his boss, Dick Scherrer, that he had found out how to make an airplane invisible, he meant that he had recognized that it was possible to design an airplane that was made entirely out of flat surfaces, canted and rotated away from the arrival angle of any radar beam.

The angles would be sharpest, and the RCS of each plate lowest, relative to the radars that could track the aircraft most efficiently—that is, the radars in front of and behind the aircraft. The side-on view is tactically less important; as an aircraft flies past a radar that is located on one side of its flightpath, the radar is directly on the airplane's beam for only a moment. The result is that most stealth aircraft have a "bow-tie" RCS picture. If you chart the RCS or detection range from above the aircraft, it blooms on both sides and is narrow at the nose and tail.

reflected from every solid object and permeates the not-quite-transparent air. A radar detects only the energy from its own transmitter, and its receiver only picks up the energy that is reflected from the target toward the radar. A radar is like a person with a flashlight, trying to find a small model airplane in a darkened auditorium.

When the focused beam of energy from a radar scans across a solid object, the electromagnetic energy is "scattered"—it bounces off in all directions, depending on the shape of the object and its arrival angle. To make life more interesting, radar waves affect the target in different ways. Some energy travels in waves along the surface, like Saint Elmo's fire. Energy is reflected when it hits the object and diffracted as the surface waves encounter creases or edges in the surface. Some of the energy is reflected toward the radar's antenna, allowing it to detect the target.

Early radar engineers soon realized that the range at which a radar could detect a target was only partly related to the target's physical size. This was a nuisance because it made it difficult to rate a radar's performance. The engineers solved the problem by developing a concept called RCS. This compares the energy reflected from a target with the energy reflected from

A subscale RCS model is readied for testing, later in the F-117 program. (It carries the 37th TFW name and insignia and the name of Colonel Al Whitley, unit commander in 1989.) *Lockheed*

If the airplane was to be made out of flat surfaces it would also have edges where they met. Again, the aircraft was designed so that those edges were swept forward or backward, away from the radar beam.

Of course, the aircraft also had to fly, which meant that it would have wings, and these wings would be flat surfaces with edges of a finite diameter. It was also a matter of basic geometry that a solid object made from surfaces sloping away from the vertical would have an edge where the upper and lower sides met, and that edge would also have a finite diameter. The edges would reflect radar more efficiently than the flat surfaces, and threatened to dominate the RCS picture.

The original Hopeless Diamond reflected two basic approaches to dealing with edges: sweep them, backward or forward, so that they are not at right angles to the most threatening radars, and make the shape out of a minimum number of long edges.

The longer the edge, the better it focuses the radar return. This may seem to be a bad thing, but consider the geometry of an aircraft with long edges passing through an area illuminated by a radar that is not directly on its flightpath. At one point only, the radar beam will be at right angles to the long leading edge, and the radar can see its echo—but the phenomenon is transient. The geometry will be less than optimal at the radar sweep before it, and less than optimal after it.

Dick Cantrell was right about the Hopeless Diamond—all the fly-by-wire in the world would not make it fly very well. Have Blue, as built and flown, reflected an important extension of edge management. In order to provide more wingspan for lift and more trailing-edge space for control, the trailing edge was notched and the wingtips were cropped, so there were more edges. But the edges were grouped along a few alignments. The left side of the exhaust assembly was parallel with the right wing trailing-edge, and vice versa. The left wingtip and the left rudder leading-edge were parallel with the right wing leading edge, and so on. This gave the designers more flexibility to produce a flyable, efficient aircraft without multiplying the RCS "spikes" around the aircraft.

So far, so good, but as Alan Brown has pointed out, "Unfortunately, these aircraft have to have engines, people flying them, et cetera." The shape was full of details where Overholser's programs provided no answers.

One of the major contributions of the Have Blue team was to develop a philosophy that governed how these features were designed and built. It centered on the recognition that RCS is not a single number but is made up of discrete elements. If a radar is not likely to detect one 0.01-square-meter object at a certain range, it is not much more likely to detect two of them. Once Overholser had calculated the RCS of the external shape, with all its complexities, spikes and troughs, what mattered was that the rest of the features had the same or lower RCS at each angle.

In the case of Have Blue, the management of apertures was primitive and inefficient, and most of it hinged on the use of RAM. There are, says Overholser, four things that you can use to reduce RCS: "shape, shape, shape, and materials." The early lesson from the U-2 "dirty bird" project still holds true—there is no RAM that is magic enough to hide a badly shaped airplane. Conversely, there is no shaping technique yet devised that can yield a practical stealth airplane without RAM. Much of the improvement in stealth technology since the days of Have Blue focuses on making better types of RAM and using it more efficiently.

The early surface coatings developed by Lockheed comprise ferromagnetic particles—the best for most applications—embedded in a high-dielectric-constant plastic. "The dielectric material slows the wave down, and the ferromagnetic particles absorb the energy," says Brown. However, Lockheed also designed its coatings so that the small reflection from the front face of the absorber is canceled by a residual reflection from the structure beneath it. The first step is to "make the total pathway [of energy within the RAM] equal to half a wavelength" so that the residual reflection is exactly out-of-phase with the front-face reflection.

The RAM can be much thinner than the nominal wavelength of the radar and still achieve cancellation, because the wavelength inside the material is much shorter than it is in free space. Also, refraction within the RAM keeps the internal path length close to constant over a wide range of incidence angles.

Finally, the absorption of the RAM is tailored so that the energy, which travels through the RAM, bounces off the substructure, and escapes, is exactly equal in magnitude to the front-face reflection. Alan Brown's comment that RAM design is "much more tricky than you would think at first sight" is a classic understatement.

Solid RAM coatings cover a frequency range of about 20:1. This is enough to address air-to-air and surface-to-air missile radars (from the L-band up to the Ku-band) but more elaborate schemes are used to cover the full radar spectrum, including low-frequency VHF radars such as the Soviet P-14.

The task of developing low-frequency RAM has been complicated by the fact that different radars affect the target in different ways. According to Lockheed scientist Dr. Vaughn Cable: "High frequencies have the same effect that you see when you shine a flashlight down the street and see a cat's eyes flash. At low frequencies, we consider radar as hammering the target and leaving the target in a mode that rings. It's a resonance effect."

Brown compares a typical wide-band radar-absorbent structure (RAS), used on the edges of a stealth aircraft, to "a stereo system, with a tweeter and a woofer." The "tweeter" is a high-frequency ferromagnetic absorber like the coating described above, applied over a resistive layer that reflects higher frequencies but allows low-frequency signals to pass through. Beneath this resistive layer is the low-frequency "woofer," a glass-fiber honeycomb core, treated from front to back with a steadily increasing amount of resistive material. Brown calls it "an electromagnetic shock absorber. It's very soft in front, but we still absorb pretty much all the energy inside, because we don't want the energy to hit the vertical front face of the structure."

Durability was an issue in the past, but RAM requirements spurred the development of tough dielectric plastics. "I can take part of a leading-edge section and bang it on a wood table, and the wood table will get a dent and the leading-edge won't," claimed Brown in 1991.

After radar, infrared (IR) sensors are the next most sensitive and discriminating sensors that can be used to detect aircraft. Under ideal conditions—at high altitude where the air is dry—IR sensors have a range in the high tens of miles or more. They detect heat from different parts of the aircraft, including the skin, which is heated by air friction or the sun and is invariably warmer than the sky behind it. They also detect heat from metal washed by hot exhaust gases (not only from the engine but also from the airplane's environmental control system). The strongest signature, however, is from the exhaust gas.

The classic outdoor RCS range is the "ground-bounce" type. Instead of attempting to eliminate multipath reflections from the target to the radar, the range designer exploits it by aiming the main beam at the ground and reflecting it up to the target. This also eliminates clutter behind the target. However, the path between the radar and the target has to be very smooth and flat. RCS ranges are sometimes misidentified as "mystery airfields." *Lockheed*

The first step in defeating IR detectors is to conceal the exhausts. Most stealth aircraft have a hot side (usually the top) and a cold side; on the F-117 and B-2, for example, the exhausts are on top of the body. (At the Farnborough air show in 1996, British Aerospace missile salesmen hyped the performance of their IR sensor, which had "detected" the B-2—but they had aimed it at the B-2's hot side as the bomber banked around the airfield.)

The next step is to shape the exhaust plume so that it cools quickly after it leaves the airplane. The AQM-91 Firefly drone was one of the first aircraft to feature an exhaust mixer nozzle, blending cool air with the hot gas to reduce its temperature. On aircraft with turbofan engines, it is important to mix the cool fan exhaust with the hotter gases from the core; otherwise, the cool air tends to insulate and stabilize the hot core exhaust, while allowing its IR radiation to pass through it. A circular nozzle produces a circular plume that retains heat, because it has the smallest possible surface area relative to its volume. Squeezing the exhaust through a flat, narrow nozzle produces a mixed plume with a large surface area, which cools quickly.

Airframe radiation—whether caused by solar or friction heating—can be reduced with the use of infrared suppressing paints and coatings. Paints containing compounds such as zinc sulfide have been developed to suppress reflections from the airplane's skin. They work like any paint, absorbing energy in a certain waveband, in this case, IR radiation from sunlight. Low-IR paints are now widely used on many different aircraft. At one point, Lockheed Martin even coated a 747 with this material, reducing its IR signature tenfold.

Paint cannot eliminate heat generated by skin friction, but special coatings can change the "emissivity" of the surface—that is, the efficiency with which it transforms heat into IR radiation. Only certain bands of IR radiation travel efficiently through the atmosphere, so the goal is to concentrate IR radiation outside those bands and let the atmosphere soak it up. By the early 1990s, coatings had been developed that would reduce the IR emissivity of any target by a factor of 10, without adding significant weight or detracting from the effectiveness of RAM coatings.

In daylight, moonlight, or even starlight, an aircraft may not be visible at any great distance—but its streaming white contrail, miles long and tens of feet across, cannot be missed. Contrail suppression is vital to any LO aircraft. The simplest approach to contrail avoidance is to fly at altitudes where they do not form. At low altitudes, the air is too warm to form contrails (the water in the trail evaporates before it freezes) and at high altitudes, the air is too dry. Contrails are relatively rare above 60,000 feet or below 20,000 feet; the high-flying U-2 normally cruises above contrail height, and the B-2 bomber has a specially developed pilot alert system, using a laser radar, which detects contrails behind the bomber and allows the pilot to adjust the aircraft's altitude until the contrails disappear.

Some aircraft, however, are not as flexible in terms of altitude performance. In that case, the best-known approach is to add a chemical to the exhaust that breaks the water down into small particles—"hypernucleation"—that are smaller than the wavelength of visible light. In the 1960s, the U.S. Air Force experimented with chlorosulfonic acid, injecting the material into the exhausts of B-47 bombers, B-52s, and AQM-34 Firebee reconnaissance drones. It was also employed on the AQM-91 Firefly drone and was to have been used on the B-2. It worked, but the material is corrosive and hazardous. More recently, Scipar has proposed using an alcohol-surfactant mixture—the company has recommended the use of Sparkleen, a commercial glass cleaner—to accomplish the same effects.

Once the long white arrow pointing to the airplane has been removed, there is some point in making the aircraft itself less visible. Military aircraft have used camouflage since World War I. The effects have usually been zero or negative, because the camouflage schemes have been designed by people who do not understand how the human eye and brain work to detect objects at a distance.

There are still air forces out there that paint airplanes green.

The first and cheapest approach to visual stealth comprises camouflage paint, and the first goal is to minimize contrast between the aircraft and the sky. Altitude is fundamental. For example, an airliner at its cruising height always appears brightly lit against the sky, regardless of its color, because both the aircraft and the sky are illuminated by light that is scattered by dust and moisture in the air. There is not much of either in the thin air above the aircraft, and lots of both below it.

The higher the altitude, the more light is scattered on to its underside, the darker the sky behind it and the darker the undersurface shade must be. Even the jet-black SR-71 and U-2 look brighter than the sky when they cruise at 80,000 feet. At lower altitudes, the sky is brighter and there is less light-scattering atmosphere below the aircraft, so lighter colors provide the least contrast. The B-2, cruising at 50,000 feet, has dark gray undersurfaces, while the F-22 has a medium-gray basic color, reflecting the altitudes at which air combat is most likely to take place. Had the Air Force not overruled the engineers, the underside of the F-117 could have been almost white.

The next step involves deceptive multitoned schemes. The objective is to confuse the eye or an optical seeker by creating false edges and suppressing real edges, so that while the image may be large enough and have sufficient contrast to be detected, it may not be recognizable as an aircraft. Research has pointed to some basic principles: areas of a single tone should not be too large, and tones in adjacent bands should differ by less than 10 percent. This is visible in the latest F-22 scheme, with irregular, slightly darker patches of gray on its wing and tail surfaces.

However, researchers since the earliest days of military aviation have attempted to do better. In World War I, German designers modified Fokker fighters and at least one heavy bomber with transparent Cellon skins, in an attempt to make them less visible. The effect was more spectral than stealthy. The material was opaque when viewed at an angle, and it glinted in the sun. Pilots could see the "invisible" aircraft about as well as they could see conventional aircraft.

In the early 1940s, a breakthrough project pointed the way to a much better solution. The intent of Project Yehudi, which was highly secret at the time and came to light only in the 1980s, was to give Navy patrol aircraft a better chance of sinking enemy submarines. During 1942, German U-boats took a heavy toll on merchant marine shipping off the East Coast of the United States. Aircraft were launched to patrol coastal waters, but submarine captains would spot the attacking aircraft and call for a crash dive. By the time the aircraft reached the submarine's last surface location, it would have lost track of its quarry.

Yehudi's inventors recognized that no camouflage paint would work. Regardless of its color, the airplane would be a black dot against the typical Atlantic sky—cloudy and backlit. The paradoxical truth was that the only way to reduce the contrast and make the airplane less visible was to light it up like a Christmas tree.

A portly TBM-3D Avenger torpedo-bomber was fitted with 10 sealed-beam lights, installed along the wing leading edges and the rim of the engine cowling. By adjusting the intensity of the lights to match the sky behind it, the Avenger would blend into the sky. Tests proved that the Yehudi system lowered the visual acquisition range from 12 miles to 2 miles, allowing the Avenger to get into striking distance of its target before it submerged. A B-24 Liberator bomber was also modified, with similar results.

Yehudi was not put into production, because better radar allowed the airplane to detect the submarine at long range and regain the tactical advantage. However, the principle was revived after air battles over Vietnam. Concerned that the big F-4 Phantom could be seen at a greater range than its much smaller Russian adversary, the MiG-21, the Pentagon started a program called Compass Ghost. An F-4 was modified with a blue-white color scheme and nine high-intensity lamps on the wings and body. Detection range was reduced by 10–30 percent with the lights on.

The Yehudi principle may be used on some operational aircraft today. For example, the first thing that a pilot sees of an F-16 is usually the shadow of the inlet duct. Lights in the duct would significantly reduce the visual acquisition range at a modest cost. As noted in the previous chapter, Have Blue was originally intended to demonstrate visual stealth, but that plan was abandoned after the loss of the prototypes. Instead, the operational F-117 controls its visual signature in the most basic manner possible, by flying only at night.

Actually, there is one type of signature that will give away an airplane's presence, position, and identity at even greater range than radar: its own electronic emissions. The importance of this signature was recognized during World War II. Late in the war, the Royal Air Force had equipped its bombers with a tail-warning radar, code-named Monica, to warn the crews of an approaching night-fighter, and the H2S radar to map targets on the ground. The Luftwaffe equipped its fighters with two passive radar receivers: Flensburg to detect Monica signals and Naxos to pick up H2S emissions. A combined system, Naxburg, was added to air-defense ground radar sites.

In July 1944, a German night-fighter crew made an elementary navigation error and landed its fully equipped aircraft at an RAF base. British analysts immediately found the Flensburg device and realized how dangerous it was. The RAF promptly removed the Monica radars and instructed crews to limit their use of H2S. In postwar tests, the British discovered that the Naxburg device had allowed German fighter controllers to observe and track bombers before they had left British airspace.

For a stealth aircraft, the lesson is that electronic emissions must be minimized or eliminated. The most straightforward technique, used on the F-117, is to do without a radar. Indeed, the F-117 would have been of little practical use, except as a reconnaissance aircraft, without the IR sensor technology developed during the Vietnam War. Even in the early days of stealth, however, radar companies were working on a group of technologies known as "low probability of intercept," or LPI.

As in the case of RCS reduction, the goal of LPI is not to be invisible or silent but to make sure that the system's emissions are not recognized for what they are. LPI techniques basically involve controlling the power, waveform, duration, frequency, and direction of radar signals to achieve two goals. The first is to use the radar to detect and track targets in the way that the system and the mission requires, while using the least possible amount of energy. The second is to inject enough apparent randomness into the signal to prevent any listening device from recognizing it.

Dr. Thomas Amlie, a Pentagon critic of stealth, has argued that any attempt to make radar less detectable is similar to "trying to hide an elephant in a strawberry patch by painting its toenails red." Amlie's observation is correct to a point. LPI technology on its own will not solve the problem. It is not enough to make the radar quiet; it is important to make less use of the radar. Any stealth aircraft must use passive sensors—whether IR or electronic—and gather targeting information via datalinks from other platforms, using active radar as a last resort.

A final and crucially important element of achieving stealth is tactical planning. This was an important lesson that emerged from the "Red

The riskiest feature of the F-117 design, aerodynamically speaking, was the canted butterfly tail. The vertical surfaces were too small as designed, and presented structural challenges when they were enlarged. *Lockheed*

Team" study of stealth, which the Pentagon commissioned in 1980. "There were elements of the operational community who bought into the idea that it was an invisible airplane that could operate with complete impunity," recalls Paul Kaminski, who headed the Red Team effort. "That was not accurate."

Developing a mission plan that minimizes the chances of being tracked is crucial to any military operation. Stealth adds a new dimension to the problem because the airplane's RCS, and hence the detection range of the hostile radars, varies with the radar's bearing—and therefore changes constantly and sometimes very significantly, as the aircraft flies. The results may be counterintuitive. Often, the best approach to a radar is nose-on, where its RCS is smallest. If the mission penetrates an overlapping array of radars of different types, the planning problem becomes extremely complicated, and is almost impossibly time-consuming if it has to be done manually.

Stealth operations, therefore, depend on the ability to map radar threats accurately and to load this map—the "electronic order of battle" or EOB—into a computerized mission planning system. Ideally, the aircraft will also have its own passive electronic sensor systems and an onboard computer system that will update the mission plan in the event that the airplane encounters an unexpected threat radar.

Most of these principles were formulated in the first few years of stealth research, before any operational aircraft had been built. Principles are one thing, and making airplanes work is another; that is the fundamental reason why it took only 5 years of development to field the first stealth combat aircraft, and almost 20 years to develop the second.

Chapter 4

BUILDING THE STEALTH FIGHTER

By the time that Lockheed's Have Blue prototype made its first flight in December 1977, the potential of stealth had been recognized at the highest levels. President Jimmy Carter's administration had reached Washington earlier that year, after the full-scale RCS tests at RATSCAT in New Mexico and Gray Butte in California had indicated that stealth technology would create massive gaps in the interlocked rings of radar coverage around Eastern Europe and the Soviet Union.

Carter's new deputy secretary of defense for research and engineering, Dr. William Perry, quickly took a strong interest in stealth. An electronics engineer by vocation, and the founder of a company producing electronic intelligence equipment, Perry recognized the potential of stealth. One of Perry's first actions on stealth was to appoint USAF Colonel Paul Kaminski, also an electronics expert, "to serve as his technical conscience," as Kaminski puts it. "Was it real or not?" Kaminski's report was positive. The next step was more difficult. Assuming that Have Blue worked, how should stealth be used?

Some high-level discussions followed in the spring of 1977, involving Perry; General Al Slay—the chief of USAF research and development; General Robert Bond, a rising Air Force star who later died while flying a MiG at Area 51, and a small support group that included two majors, Ken Staton and Joe Ralston. (In 2000, the latter is vice-chairman of the Joint Staff.)

One option studied by the group was whether the potential of stealth was so explosive that the technology should be shut down, the programs stopped, and the data locked away, Ralston remarked at a conference in 1990. The Soviet Union was showing a disconcerting tendency to develop new generations of weapons on a shorter cycle than the United States, and to field them more quickly once developed. Stealth did not discriminate between U.S. and Soviet radars. The concern was that, once the idea of stealth became public, Soviet researchers would uncover its secrets and render U.S. air defenses useless. But Perry, as Kaminski recalls, "thought it was better to run fast than to behave like an ostrich."

The study group looked at how stealth could be applied to any type of conflict, ranging from counterinsurgency operations, through regional and European conventional conflict, to nuclear deterrence. Conventional warfare and nuclear deterrence were seen as the missions in which stealth would provide the greatest military advantage.

The first F-117 in final assembly at Burbank. Some cockpit assembly has started but the inlets and jetpipes, which are separate subassemblies, have not yet been installed. *Lockheed*

The F-117 was basically of conventional aluminum skin-and-stringer construction. The centerbody, seen here, held almost all the fuel, the engines, and the weapon bays. *Lockheed*

Next, the Pentagon group examined what kind of stealth combat aircraft could be developed for a reasonable level of risk. using Have Blue technology. "Two or three things were obvious," says Alan Brown. "We had relatively poor performance because of our very low-aspect-ratio planform. We could not fly very far, and we were clearly not agile or maneuverable." An attack or bomber design was much more practical than an air-combat fighter.

The next question was how large the operational aircraft should be. The basic decisions concerned range, payload, the number of crew on board, and equipment. A large airplane with a pilot and weapon system officer (WSO) and a radar would be more flexible than a simpler single-seat aircraft, and could be used against more targets in more difficult conditions. On the other hand, it would take longer and cost more to develop, and there was a greater risk of delay failure. Pushing for more capability could result in no capability.

One concept that attracted much attention was the idea that a small number of stealth aircraft could attack the enemy air defense system, allowing a larger force of conventional aircraft to get through with acceptable losses. The Pentagon leaders "were sold on the force multiplier effect, on 'silver bullet' aircraft," says Brown.

Much of the uniformed Air Force preferred a larger aircraft. In the summer of 1977, Carter and his defense secretary, Harold Brown, canceled the USAF's B-1A bomber. (It was resurrected by the Reagan administration four years later, as the B-1B.) A larger stealth aircraft could take over part of the bomber's mission.

In October 1977—as the first Have Blue neared completion in Burbank—Lockheed was awarded a contract to look at two versions of what was now

Right
When the F-117 was still deadly secret, someone who had seen it being built remarked: "If you saw it on the production line, with the wings off, you'd know it was some kind of a vehicle and you'd know which direction it was designed to go in, but you wouldn't think it was an airplane." *Lockheed*

47

The first flying F-117 was given the number 780 (for the month and year of its scheduled first flight) so the static test airframe was 779. Here, the centerbody of 779 undergoes a strength test. *Lockheed*

Opposite
A crowded F-117 assembly line at Burbank in the 1980s. In the foreground, aft fuselages are being attached; the midbody sections are being assembled in the center, and wings are being fabricated on the far side of the hangar. There were few major subcontractors for the airframe, which Lockheed built almost from scratch. *Lockheed*

known as the Advanced Tactical Aircraft (ATA). The "A" version was the low-risk scale-up of the Have Blue; the "B" was much larger, around the size of the FB-111 bomber, with a two-member crew. "We had much less confidence that we could pull that design off," Ralston commented in 1990. "There were some tough decisions that had to be made by a small group of people." One critical issue was whether or not a single pilot could perform the mission envisaged for the smaller aircraft. "We flew a simulator and found one person could do it."

The A and B designs were defined in early 1978. They were similar in shape, and both closely resembled Have Blue. The A airplane was designed around two General Electric F404 engines, as used on the navy's F/A-18 Hornet fighter, and could carry two 2,000-pound bombs on a 400-nautical-mile mission radius. The two-seat B airplane weighed 90,000 pounds and was powered by two GE F101s, as developed for the B-1. It would carry 7,500 pounds of weapons and have a mission radius of 1,000 nautical miles.

The decision was complex. The larger bomber would be more useful and was estimated to cost only 50 percent more than the smaller airplane. Denys Overholser—now nicknamed "the Wizard of Oz" by his colleagues—was confident that he could add some one-dimensional curvature to the external shape, reducing RCS and drag. The improved lift-to-drag ratio would make it easier to design a longer-range aircraft; without the aerodynamic refinements, the take-off and landing characteristics of the heavier B airplane would be marginally acceptable. But, says Brown, "we wouldn't be able to calculate the improvement." The customer vetoed the changes on the grounds of risk.

Ralston and his colleagues in the small LO office became convinced that the B airplane was not the way to go after they "flew" the design in Lockheed's engineering simulator. Ralston and two colleagues each attempted five take-offs. Ralston saved the airplane once but the other take-off attempts resulted in the loss of the aircraft.

While Strategic Air Command remained enthusiastic for the larger aircraft, the LO group argued convincingly that the smaller aircraft would present enough novelties and challenges—a view that was confirmed by later events. Senior Air Force leaders accepted this argument, and by the summer of 1978 they decided to go ahead with the ATA A version. (The larger aircraft was not dead, though; it evolved very quickly into a design for a stealth strategic bomber, which would be developed later using knowledge gained in testing of the smaller aircraft.) In November 1978, Lockheed was awarded a contract to carry out full-scale development (FSD) of the A aircraft. The program was code-named Senior Trend.

Lockheed would build five FSD aircraft while starting an initial batch of 20 production aircraft, and the goal was to fly the first aircraft in July 1980 and achieve initial operational capability (IOC) in March 1982. The most important elements of the specification concerned RCS and weapon delivery accuracy, but the overriding need was for secrecy. As far as possible, the existence of the airplane was to be kept secret, even after it entered service.

The secrecy, the airplane's basic characteristics, and the small number of aircraft were all influenced by the airplane's intended mission and its most important targets. During the 1970s, the Soviet Union had developed and expanded an integrated air defense system (IADS) in Central Europe. In the event of a large-scale conventional war in Europe, NATO commanders knew that their best hope for survival was to use airpower to sever the advancing Soviet land forces from the stream of supplies, reinforcements, and spares that they would need in order to keep moving. The IADS, intended to protect Soviet forces while destroying NATO aircraft, comprised thousands of surface-to-air missile launchers and radars, cued by long-range radars and tied together by computerized control centers.

The system's reliance on central control was a potential weakness, but the control centers were heavily defended and invulnerable to conventional attack. An unexpected attack by the Senior Trend aircraft could knock the entire IADS off balance. "The principal targets," said a 1979 requirements document, "will be command, control and communications centers, air

defense facilities, airfields, logistics choke points and other targets of high military value."

From the start of the program, the USAF planned to buy more than 20 aircraft; Lockheed's plans envisaged that as many as 100 might be built. The first aircraft would carry IR sensors for clear-weather night attack, but an LPI radar would also be developed for the aircraft. The first aircraft would be armed with laser-guided bombs, but the aircraft was also designed to carry missiles, including air-to-air missiles (AAMs) for use against Soviet airborne early-warning and control (AEW&C) aircraft.

The Senior Trend aircraft strongly resembled Have Blue. The overall layout was the same, with sharply swept wings, a broad body, and flat underside. The inlet and exhaust configuration was basically similar. There were some basic differences that reflected lessons learned in the Have Blue program. The Senior Trend's wing was less sharply swept, sac-

Wings removed, canopy masked, and fitted with a tie-down adapter, the world's first operational stealth airplane is shrouded for its journey from Burbank to Area 51, in the summer of 1981. *Lockheed*

rificing some head-on RCS performance but increasing its span, which improved aerodynamic efficiency and made room for two elevon surfaces on each side. The changes made it possible to eliminate the platypus flap, which had brought about the demise of the first Have Blue. The inward-canted rudders, which had proven only marginally effective, were replaced by a butterfly tail attached to the apex of the afterbody.

One characteristic feature of the Senior Trend's shape was a response to a problem on Have Blue, the difficulty of maintaining a perfect seal on doors and other apertures. The solution was to align the edges of all the apertures with the edges of the airplane, and to make sure that they were all swept at least 45 degrees from the head-on aspect. Some apertures, including the cockpit and weapon bays, were bounded by internal transverse bulkheads; in these cases, the doors were given a saw-toothed shape.

The careful alignment of the internal and external edges, combined with 2,000 pounds of RAM, had an important benefit. The aircraft would retain its low-RCS properties, even if assembly was not perfect. Alan Brown remarks that Lockheed could not afford to be too sophisticated. "We needed 1,200 people to build it, and we couldn't get them from the main plant because they were all working on other programs." A few miles from Burbank, however, Ford was closing an auto plant at Pico Rivera, and most of

In the dead of night, a Lockheed C-5A is prepared to carry the ultrasecret prototype to its flight-test location—a base so sensitive that its identity remains a secret more than 40 years after it was established. *Lockheed*

the new workers came from there. "They had not built aircraft before, they didn't have clearances, and it was hard to get them cleared because of drug usage." (In late-1970s Los Angeles, the last problem was not unusual.) Net result: Lockheed could not afford to be choosy about its people, and "couldn't afford to build anything that required the skills of Swiss watchmakers."

Another new feature of Senior Trend was its weapon-delivery system, which was designed to deliver iron bombs with reasonable accuracy and laser-guided bombs (LGBs) with much greater precision. To take full advantage of the LGB's accuracy, it also gave the pilot a means to select a precise aimpoint on the target. To save time, Lockheed designed the weapon-delivery system around existing components. The engineers and the program office also accepted that the system at IOC would be less than ideal, and that it would be upgraded later.

For en-route navigation, the fighter used the Honeywell SPN/GEANS (Standard Precision Navigator / Gimbaled Electrically Aircraft Navigation System), which had originally been developed for the B-52's Offensive Avionics System (OAS) upgrade program. This was a complex inertial navigation system in which the platform carrying the gyroscopes and accelerometers was suspended electrostatically, rather than mechanically. Its crucial advantage was a drift rate—loss of accuracy with time—that was lower than any other INS of the time.

The INS would place the fighter close enough to the target for the infrared acquisition and designation system (IRADS) to take over. Developed by Texas Instruments, the IRADS was built from existing components (such as turrets, coolers, and optics) but was configured to meet the unique requirements of the stealth fighter. Earlier IR systems had been carried in large external pods so that their optical turrets could scan a large field of view around the aircraft, but such an arrangement was incompatible with stealth. On the other hand, there was no way to build a single IR turret in the skin so that it would have an acceptable field of view. The solution was a compromise with two turrets—a forward-looking IR (FLIR) located in front of the windshield and a downward-looking IR (DLIR) installed to the left of the nosewheel bay—controlled by a common processor set and providing imagery to a large video display (taken from the Navy's P-3 patrol aircraft). The system was arranged so that the fighter would fly directly over the target to attack it, giving the weapon a short trajectory and making it more accurate. The DLIR was fitted with a laser designator.

The original weapon delivery computer (WDC) subsystem used the same Delco M362F computers as the F-16. The computers tied together the INS, the IRADS, and the cockpit controls and displays, and could be loaded with mission data using an electronic data cartridge system in the cockpit. The IRADS imagery on the main tactical display was stored on a video recorder.

The entire Senior Trend weapon-delivery system was designed to be largely automatic. The INS would guide the aircraft toward the target using the mission plan loaded via the data cartridge, and would then aim the FLIR at the target. The pilot's task was to find the target in the FLIR image and place a cross-hair over it. An autotracker in the FLIR would hold the system on that aimpoint. As the airplane approached the target, the IRADS would automatically cue the DLIR onto it and continue tracking. The pilot would confirm the target and depress the trigger to consent to weapon release, but the computers would actually time the release of the weapon and activate the laser. It was as far from a white-scarf fighter-pilot mission as it was possible to get. (In fact, when the idea of an uninhabited combat air vehicle or UCAV was mooted in the mid-1990s, it was suggested that the F-117 would be the best basis for a demonstrator.)

Despite the tight security surrounding the stealth project, some information had leaked to the aviation trade press. In its early days, stealth was not highly classified, and it was not surprising that reporters covering technology issues inside the Pentagon picked up news of what was going on. *Aviation Week* accurately reported in January 1976 that Lockheed and Northrop had been working on a stealth fighter program. In July, three months after DARPA awarded the Have Blue contract to Lockheed, *Aerospace Daily* reported that Lockheed had won a contract to build a 12,000-pound test aircraft.

Stealth started to receive more public attention in 1979–1980—not because of the Have Blue project, but because of political controversy. In the run-up to the 1980 elections, Republicans accused President Carter

of allowing U.S. forces to become weak, and a series of intelligence leaks pointed to new and threatening Soviet developments in missiles and fighters.

The USAF had resumed studies of a new manned bomber: the three options were a revived B-1, a much-modified FB-111, and the Lockheed stealth bomber, which had emerged from the ATA B design. Press reports in 1980 suggested that a stealthy bomber could be in service by 1987. In August 1980, Defense Secretary Harold Brown confirmed the existence of a stealth program, without saying anything specific about Have Blue or acknowledging that the Senior Trend aircraft was under development. In 1981, however, *Aviation Week* reported correctly that Lockheed was building 20 stealth fighters and that they were about the size of the F/A-18.

At the same time, the ring-fence of security around stealth became larger. As it became clear that stealth was a practical and valuable technology, other aircraft manufacturers formed stealth design teams. They were not privy to the secrets of Have Blue, but they were dealing with the same physics and the same public data that Lockheed and Northrop had used. There was clearly a chance that another company would replicate a crucial feature of the new technology outside the Special Access controls. In 1981, for instance, a team of Grumman engineers presented a paper to a Society of Automotive Engineers conference that described a stealthy attack aircraft in detail.

In 1981–1982, the Pentagon virtually banned any public discussion of stealth by anyone who worked for the government or its contractors. (In 1985, I needed a copy of the 1981 Grumman paper, and visited the engineering library at Berkeley in California. I turned to the correct page in the library's bound volume of the 1981 SAE proceedings—and the offending paper was missing, neatly excised with a sharp instrument.)

The Pentagon managed to drag a ripe red herring across the trail in 1981, when the USAF allocated the designation F-20 to Northrop's Tigershark fighter. The logical assumption was that the stealth fighter was the F-19, since the last known designation was F/A-18 and the Pentagon nomenclature system does not normally skip numbers (except –13). However, the Pentagon could and did deny that the F-19 existed; Senior Trend was the F-117.

The basis for this designation has never been revealed, but the most plausible explanation is that it was an extension of a series of designations used for the Soviet aircraft that were tested at Area 51. At least two official biographies of senior USAF and Navy officers who flew with the 4477th Test and Evaluation Squadron—the Red Hats or Red Eagles, based at Area 51—list "YF-110" and "YF-113" among the aircraft that their subjects have flown. Since the F-117 was to be based on the Nellis range, the designation

The canopy has been reinstalled and the unique tailpipes have been put in place, but some skin panels are still removed and the aircraft has not been painted. Camouflage nets cover the open hangar door. *Lockheed*

served as a double cover. First, the entire designation series referred to a classified program, and second, anyone seeing the designation would have no way of knowing that it referred to a U.S.-built aircraft.

As for the F-19: the best guess is that there was no F-19, and that the number was skipped to give the Tigershark a fresher designation—the first fighter of the 1980s, rather than the last of the 1970s—as a favor from the Reagan administration to Northrop Chairman Tom Jones.

Secrecy concealed delays and problems from public view. The F-117 was a complex system that included a number of new components, which were crucial to its ability to perform a combat mission. The FSD program encountered a series of technical problems related to such vital issues. Combined with labor shortages and a schedule that was optimistic in the first place, they caused the first flight to slip 11 months, from June 1980 to July of the following year.

The F-117's basic external shape was sound, and it performed largely as expected in terms of RCS and aerodynamics. However, some large and important parts of the aircraft, where stealth had driven the designers to unusual solutions, gave serious trouble. The tailpipes were a problem from

the start. Under heat and pressure, the upper and lower skins of the flattened tailpipes were under great and uneven stress, leading to failures during tests. The final design of the tailpipe and afterbody was complex. Cooled vertical struts in the tailpipe connected the upper and lower surfaces and resisted the tendency to bulge outward. The platypus was designed with skins that overlapped, so that it could expand and contract without warping, and parts of the exhaust were covered with the same heat-resistant tiles as the Space Shuttle.

The inlets, as Alan Brown put it later, "not only looked like ice-cube trays but acted that way." The problem was that no conventional means of de-icing the inlets—whether using inflatable boots, hot air, or electrical heating—was both effective and compatible with stealth. The final solution was a retractable mechanical wiper system, stowed in a step beneath the inlet, which sprayed de-icing fluid over the inlet grid. The wipers are operated by the pilot, who watches for ice formation with the aid of a small light on either side of the fuselage.

Another difficult problem was providing a screen for the IRADS apertures. The canopy transparencies were coated with a layer of indium-tin oxide (ITO), which reflected radar signals (since the windows were sharply angled, their contribution to RCS was not significant), but ITO also blocked IR radiation. The designers initially planned to use a zinc-selenide crystal material for the IRADS covers. The crystals had to be individually grown over a six-month period until they could be shaped into the screens, and cost $300,000 apiece. "The first one we installed cracked straight across the middle," Brown recalls.

By March 1982, not one workable screen had been delivered. Over a weekend, Brown devised a substitute that was not a transparent screen but a very fine wire mesh, a "high tensile tennis racquet." It admitted 70 to 75 percent of visible and IR radiation, blocked radar signals and, apart from some residual acoustic vibration, acted as a solid surface to the airflow. It was adopted as a short-term fix and remains in use to this day.

The single thorniest problem was the air-data system. As an unstable, fly-by-wire aircraft, the F-117 could not fly safely without an accurate system to measure speed, angle of attack, and sideslip. The system also needed four independent channels, so that even if one channel failed in flight the system would still be able to detect a problem in any of the other channels using a simple "voting" logic. The F-117 was designed with four faceted probes on its nose. The tip was a pyramid with a port in each face, and the flight attitude was calculated from the differences in pressure between the ports. As in the case of the inlets, the problem was to protect the tips from ice while retaining the system's stealth qualities. Additionally, packing multiple pressure tubes and heating wires into the probes proved difficult.

Kaminski recalls an "agonizing period in which we had three or four designs of pitot-static system on the F-117." For a time, Kaminski says, the designers were working with different systems that each met some but not all of these vital requirements. A small team hand-built the experimental probes. The problem was not resolved until late in the flight-test program, and failure would have rendered the aircraft unusable.

Some of these problems had not been solved when the first aircraft flew from Area 51 on June 18, 1981. (It carried the tail code 780. This signified the month and year of the scheduled first flight date, and remaining aircraft followed in sequence.) The flight lasted 14 minutes, and showed that the directional stability was inadequate; by October, 780 was equipped with larger vertical tails. Four of the five FSD aircraft were flying by April 1982; the fifth was complete but was undergoing preparation for RCS tests, and 785, the first production aircraft, was being prepared for flight tests.

Lockheed test pilot Bob Ridenauer attempted the first flight of aircraft 785 on April 20, 1982. As Ridenauer rotated the aircraft for takeoff, it yawed and pitched violently and landed on its back. Ridenauer was injured but survived. It did not take long to determine that the pitch and yaw channels in the flight control system had been cross-connected. When the airplane rotated for take-off, the computers interpreted the movement as an uncommanded yaw, and corrected it with the rudders. The airplane yawed in response to the rudders, and the computers detected an uncommanded pitch movement, and moved the elevons to

Reassembly complete, aircraft 780 is ready for its first flight. Problems with the forward-looking infrared window have not yet been solved, and a dummy screen is installed instead. A conventional nose probe carries air-data sensors, because the stealthy system based on four pyramid-tipped probes has not been made to work. *Lockheed*

oppose it. The catastrophic miswiring sparked an investigation of the program, which led to more delays.

Flight tests continued. The major problems with the probes, inlets, and other features were on the top of the agenda, but other issues—such as the performance of the IRADS—continued to pose challenges. Moreover, the aircraft needed more maintenance than expected, slowing the progress of the test program.

The first FSD aircraft carried a multitone camouflage scheme like that borne by the first Have Blue, designed to conceal its shape from satellite photo interpreters. It was later repainted in a light gray scheme, fading to lighter shades underneath, which Scipar had designed for Lockheed. It was a carefully designed scheme, and reduced visual detection range under a variety of night conditions (moonlight and clouds lit by ground lighting, for example) as well as in daylight.

Senior USAF commanders, including Tactical Air Command leader General William Creech, ordered a change to an all-black scheme. The change has been ascribed to aesthetics—"Trainers are white, and real fighters are black"—but one source has suggested that Creech had a reason for making the change. Creech "did not think that the airplane could ever survive in daylight," the source suggests, "and by painting them black he made sure that nobody would use them that way." In any event, the commanders were well aware that black was the worst possible color for the F-117. "It stands out like an ink blot in any ambient light," says Alan Brown. "At least,

Hal Farley made the first flight of the F-117 on June 18, 1981. The aircraft turned out to be directionally unstable. Lockheed engineers had anticipated the problem and provided Farley with a switch that allowed him to quickly increase the stability augmentation provided by the flight control computers. *Lockheed*

it took us off the hook for the visual signature specifications." (How bad is black for a stealth aircraft? In the 1990s, the Royal Air Force determined that black was the best color for their trainers, because it made them more visible and reduced the risk of midair collisions.)

Delays and uncertainties played a part in causing production plans to fluctuate in the early 1980s. As early as 1980, the USAF was planning to buy a wing of F-117s, rather than a single squadron. By the end of 1981, the USAF was looking at acquiring a total of 89 production aircraft. Later aircraft would be F-117Bs, featuring a radar and provision for AGM-88 High-speed Anti-Radiation Missiles (HARMs). However, the continuing test problems meant that money had to be transferred from production to fund extra development work on the basic F-117A. By late 1982, the program was established at a goal of 57 aircraft (59 production aircraft were eventually completed). All of them would be F-117As, but some of the money that would have paid for an F-117B was used for more modest improvements to the aircraft.

The USAF was still determined to field a few operational stealth fighters as soon as possible. The first stealth unit, the 4450th Tactical Group, had been formed in October 1979. Lacking aircraft, it initially comprised a core group of pilots and maintainers who helped guide the program and provided advice on operational requirements, while preparing for service entry at the F-117's new base.

Area 51 was unsuitable for an operational base, because it housed other classified programs. The 4450th could not train pilots for a 20-aircraft unit if it had to suspend operations and sequester its people whenever another program needed to fly. Consequently, the USAF decided to build an all-new base on the site of a small airstrip at Tonopah Test Range (TTR), at the northwest corner of the Nellis complex. Because TTR could be seen from public land, most flying would be carried out at night. Further cover was provided by a bogus mission and "surrogate" aircraft. Officially, the 4450th was flying Vought A-7Ds and two-seat A-7Ks for "avionics testing."

The 4450th started recruiting pilots in 1980. The unit sought out pilots with air-to-ground experience, 1,000 hours or more in flight time, and good performance ratings—many of the pilots contacted were Fighter Weapons School graduates. At their initial interviews, pilots were told that they would be flying A-7s and that the postings would separate them from their families during the week. They were given five minutes to decide whether to volunteer.

The 4450th's commanders included an unusually large proportion of "fast burners"—fighter pilots who had already been identified as future generals. (By 1997, 10 former 4450th officers had been promoted to general—a remarkable figure for a unit that was operational for only six years and never had more than 50 aircraft.)

The unit declared itself operational at the end of October 1983, with a "limited" IOC. This meant that it had 10 F-117s, 8 of which could be ready to go within 48 hours, and that it could deploy worldwide if needed. The unit was officially classified as "marginally combat ready" because of the small number of aircraft. One major system that was not yet available was the computerized Automated Mission Planning System (AMPS); threat-avoidance routes still had to be prepared by hand, taking six to eight hours per mission. Maintainability was poor; in January 1984, the F-117s required almost 113 manhours of maintenance for every hour in the air, and they were only fully mission-capable—with all stealth systems in perfect shape—for 11 percent of the time.

As more aircraft arrived, the training regime became more intense. The crews' families lived around Nellis AFB near Las Vegas, and most of the 4450th personnel commuted weekly to Tonopah by air. (A charter company, Key Airlines, was formed to operate a Boeing 727 transport with security-cleared crews.) For security reasons, all training was carried out at night. Flight-worthy aircraft usually flew two sorties with different pilots every night—"early go" and "late go." In the summer, the first "early go" jet would take off at 2230 hours and the last "late go" jet might land as late as 0300 hours. Pilots found themselves in a near-constant state of jet lag. The USAF found that daylight had an immense influence on the body clock, and the 4450th pilots were encouraged to make sure that they were in their darkened

One of the development F-117s above the Mojave desert. The operational aircraft were to have been painted in this light gray color, which is actually less visible than black under nearly all night conditions, but the engineers were overruled by Tactical Air Command leaders. *Lockheed*

living quarters before dawn. Skunk Works leader Ben Rich likened the scene to "a vampire convention . . . watching all the night workers scurrying for their blacked-out rooms before they were caught by the sun."

Early in the program, the F-117 pilots named themselves "Bandits." Each pilot had a Bandit number, assigned in sequence. The first operational squadrons were nicknamed the "Ghost Riders" and the "Grim Reapers." The most arcane nickname for the 4450th was the "Goatsuckers." The F-117 itself was unofficially called the Nighthawk (the name became official in June 1994) and "Goatsucker" is an alternative name for the North American nighthawk.

The F-117 was not a difficult aircraft to fly, and its missions did not require a wide flight envelope; the lack of a two-seat trainer version was not a problem (as it had been for the U-2 and Blackbird). The focus of the training sorties, which ventured as much as 300 miles from TTR, was on navigation, precisely following the planned course, and finding the designated target. The last task was often the most difficult. Targets were not always as obvious as the buildings that the F-117s would later attack in Desert Storm, and pilots had to learn to use nearby objects as cues to locate a less conspicuous aimpoint above a concealed target. Pilots usually practiced refueling—with no lights and no radio—at least once a week.

The first F-117 made its maiden flight in this crudely applied temporary camouflage scheme. Like the scheme used on the first Have Blue, it was designed so that the shape could not be easily discerned from satellite photographs. *Lockheed*

On training flights, the aircraft were identified to traffic controllers as A-7s. The F-117 is fitted with radar reflectors—retractable units under the fuselage and detachable reflectors on the body side—which ensure that air traffic control radars can see the aircraft and mask its true signature.

On two occasions before mid-1986, the 4450th was readied for a potential mission. (One of these was a possible strike against Libya; the other may have involved Lebanon or Grenada.) However, the order to launch was never given, and conventional aircraft were used for the Eldorado Canyon strikes against Libya in April 1986.

The nocturnal training continued, made particularly stressful by short summer nights. By Thursday, the last flying night of a routine week, "you were a wreck," one pilot recalled. But the importance of the training and the airplane's mission, combined with what Ben Rich called "the typical, macho pilot attitude that it's not manly to say you're too tired to fly" caused pilots to fly despite fatigue. Early in the morning of July 11, an F-117 flown by Major Ross Mulhare dived under full power into rough terrain near Bakersfield. Mulhare did not eject and was killed. There was no indication of mechanical failure, and investigators concluded that the pilot had become disoriented.

The crash of an airplane that the USAF refused to identify focused media attention on the stealth fighter. Photographs of the new base at Tonopah had been published. Given its long rows of small hangars, it was not too hard to guess what was happening there. But the F-117s continued to fly at night—although with more attention to pilot fatigue—and as far as is known they eluded any attempt to photograph them.

Meanwhile, Lockheed continued to work on upgrades to the F-117. The Delco computers were known from the outset to be just adequate for the F-117, and a program to replace them began in 1984. Under the Weapon System Computational Subsystem (WSCS) upgrade, IBM AP-102 computers based on 1750A standards replaced the overworked Delcos, and the aircraft were further modified (including the introduction of new composite weapon-bay doors) to allow two weapons to be released per pass. The 45th production F-117 (serial number 829), delivered in November 1987, was the first WSCS aircraft.

The F-117 also acquired a new weapon. Many of its targets were protected by concrete shelters or reinforced bunkers, and the standard 2,000-pound Mk 84 bomb was not particularly effective against them; if it was delay-fused, its rolled-steel case tended to break up on impact. Under a program called Have Void, Lockheed Missiles and Space Company developed a 2,000-pound bomb with a thick, bullet-shaped forged case of hardened steel and a tail-mounted fuse. (It was basically a baby version of the British Tallboy and Grand Slam of World War II.) It was mated to the improved seeker of the Paveway III LGB, which could guide the bomb to a vertical impact angle. The warhead was designated BLU-109, and the complete LGB is the GBU-27.

Oddly, Have Void was not classified, and the author was briefed on it at Eglin AFB in 1985. A few unstated facts were obvious. For maximum effect against a flat or near-flat surface—as bunker tops usually are—the bomb had to be released from a straight-and-level pass toward the target. The target was by definition valuable and therefore would be heavily defended. Any conventional aircraft would be shot down long before it could guide its weapon to impact. The briefers' reticence as to the intended platform for the new bomb was not surprising.

The standard F-117 test target is a 55-gallon oil drum containing a charcoal fire. In the early 1990s, the Skunk Works proudly displayed one of these 55-gallon drums, split neatly in half by an inert GBU-27 on the second test sortie of the program in early 1987.

Some of the maintainability problems were eased after 1985, when Lockheed started switching from sheet-type RAM to a more durable sprayed-on material. Another change concerned the vertical tail surfaces, which had been enlarged hastily to correct the lack of directional stability encountered on the first flight. The rudders were known to have a lower flutter limit than the originals, resulting in a speed restriction to Mach 0.8. In September 1985, USAF test pilot Jon Beesley was performing a weapons test when one of the vertical tails fluttered "explosively" and separated. Beesley recovered the aircraft, and a program was started to develop a new tail using thermoplastic/graphite composite material. The F-117 made its first flight with the new tail in July 1989.

Forward fuselage of the first F-117, call sign Scorpion 1. The gridded inlets were installed from the start of flight tests, but the de-icing system—located in a step below the inlet—was introduced later. Skip Anderson was Lockheed's lead pilot on the program. *Lockheed*

By late 1988, pressure to declassify the aircraft was increasing. Many of the F-117's growing pains were in the past. The WSCS aircraft was in service and was significantly better in terms of workload and accuracy than the initial standard. The automated mission planning system was working; the pilots had dubbed it "Elvira," after TV's *Mistress of the Dark*. More than 50 of the planned 59 production aircraft had been delivered. With so many aircraft and pilots, the ban on daylight operations was an increasingly onerous constraint on training. (Another fatal accident had occurred in October 1987, under similar conditions to the 1986 crash.)

Also, the Northrop B-2 stealth bomber was ready to be rolled out. The B-2 had never literally been a "black" program, and the USAF had always accepted that it would be tested in daylight from Edwards AFB. Lockheed grumbled that its own program remained under wraps, but had achieved far more than its rival's efforts. "We're like the rabbi who scores a hole in one on a Saturday," complained Ben Rich.

Acknowledging the F-117 would also allow U.S. theater commanders to build the aircraft into their war plans. Again, this was less important when there were only a handful of F-117s in service; more so when the stealth fighters could take on a significant part of the air campaign.

In early October 1988—weeks before the presidential election—it appeared that a public announcement about the F-117 might be imminent. Under intense pressure from Congressional Democrats, the announcement was delayed. A fuzzy and horribly foreshortened photograph of the F-117 was released on November 10, almost exactly 10 years after the Senior Trend program started.

The first and most dramatic effect of the disclosure was that the 4450th started flying in daylight. TTR became a tourist destination for intrepid aviation photographers, and there was no way to tell how many of them were reporting to foreign intelligence agencies. With the fighter's external shape thoroughly compromised, the USAF made the best of the inevitable and presented two F-117s in public at Nellis AFB in April 1989.

Late in 1989, the 4450th TG lost its provisional designation and became the 37th Tactical Fighter Wing. On December 21, the aircraft were used in combat for the first time, as part of the Just Cause operation to remove President Manuel Noriega from power in Panama. Since the Panama Defense Force had no means to shoot down the F-117s, this was not a test of the system's stealth capability, but of its precision. As it happened, only two bombs were released, aimed at a target next to a PDF barracks. The goal was to confuse and disorientate the Panamanian forces in advance of a ground attack. One of the bombs missed its target; later, one

The fully developed F-117 was armed with the GBU-27 laser-guided bomb, which combined either a standard Mk84 2,000-pound bomb or a BLU-109 hard-target bomb (seen here) with a guidance section. The wire-mesh screen covering the infrared targeting turret in front of the windshield is so fine as to be invisible. *Lockheed*

pilot said that he felt that the 37th TFW had "got a bum rap" because one of the bombs landed off target. "If you give a person a target, he can hit that target. Give a person a field and he can hit that field. The difficulty is what part of the field he's going to hit. It was a difficult night for everybody."

A very different campaign started in the summer of 1990, after Iraqi forces invaded Kuwait and defied demands from the United States and its allies to withdraw. Iraq had spent billions on Soviet-built air-defense hardware, and Bagdad and other key targets were considered to be as densely protected as any target in the Soviet Union or Eastern Europe. The USAF, meanwhile, saw a war against Iraq as an ideal use for massive airpower, and identified the F-117 as a key to success. A squadron of 18 F-117s arrived at King Khalid Air Base at Khamis Mushait, 6,800 feet up in the coastal mountain range near the Saudi-Yemeni border, on August 21; another 20 aircraft arrived on December 3.

The crews arrived to find first-rate facilities, including air-conditioned shelters, which were so new that the seals were still on the doors. The high-desert environment was similar to TTR. (It has been suggested that "Tonopah East" was purpose-built during the 1980s, in anticipation of a need to deploy the F-117s.) "We got there with everything

we needed," a pilot remarked later, "and if we had to, we could have gone to war the next day, which was the basic requirement. It was real nice to have the time, though."

USAF planners in the "Black Hole," the strategic planning cell in Riyadh, relied heavily on the F-117. The challenge for the planners was to use the first night's operations to damage Iraq's air defense capability beyond recovery, even in the absence of strategic surprise. The air campaign might last for weeks, and losses would mount unacceptably if the defenses remained intact. The F-117s' task on the first night was to attack air defense and command and control sites, and to destroy military-related buildings in Bagdad itself. After that, the fighters would take the lead in the campaign against Iraq's nuclear and chemical weapons facilities, as well as crucial highway bridges.

Right
Operational F-117s often fly with radar reflectors installed on their body sides. This ensures that air traffic controllers can see the aircraft even if their ATC transponders are not working, and prevents unauthorized radar operators from seeing the airplane's real radar signature. *Lockheed*

A daylight four-ship formation is the antithesis of normal F-117 operations. The airplane is full of intricate detail, including the careful alignment of the edges of all apertures with the leading or trailing edges of the wing. Weathering due to heat is visible on the exhausts, which are a heavy-maintenance item. *Lockheed*

The first F-117s launched against their targets just after midnight on January 17. Representing only 2.5 percent of the total number of fighters and bombers (shooters) available to the coalition, the F-117As attacked 31 percent of the first-day targets, including the main early-warning sites and all the downtown Bagdad targets that were hit. The latter included the main headquarters buildings, the main microwave telecommunications links, and power supplies.

Particularly over Bagdad, the F-117s arrived to face a wall of fire from missiles and guns. Operating in radio silence, some of the F-117 pilots were convinced that theirs was the only airplane from the 37th to survive—but every aircraft returned, and not one F-117 was hit during the entire campaign.

After the initial strikes, the Iraqi air defenses were getting virtually no targeting information from the lobotomized C2 system. The only way they could operate was to use their own search radars fulltime. Jamming from defensive EW equipment aboard strike aircraft and from escort jammers, however, severely reduced their ability to detect and track hostile aircraft. On the other hand, full-time transmission made them extremely vulnerable to direct attack by Wild Weasels and other aircraft with antiradiation missiles (ARMs). Within a few days, Iraqi SAM operators were using their radars for no more than 20 seconds at a time.

With the air defense campaign over, the F-117s took on other targets, such as the Iraqi nuclear weapons research site at Osirak. It had been attacked and damaged by the Israeli Air Force in 1981, and was subsequently fortified against air attack. The defenses included 300-foot earth berms surrounding the facility, topped by towers carrying cables that crossed the site. Smoke pots were installed every 15 feet along the berms. The site was also surrounded by surface-to-air missile batteries.

In the first U.S. strike, with F-16s in the attack role, the smoke pots were activated, preventing accurate weapon delivery. The defenses were intense, and one F-16 pilot reported being under attack by seven SAMs at one time. During the following day's Air Tasking Order (ATO) briefing, an F-117 pilot volunteered the 37th TFW for the target, and eight F-117s struck it that night, delivering 16 weapons and destroying 16 targets. On subsequent nights, the F-117s systematically destroyed Osirak.

Air operations ended on February 28, with the F-117 in the role of hero. However, its success in combat did not translate into new production, and Desert Storm represented the zenith of the type's importance. In June 1992, the F-117 wing moved to Holloman AFB, New Mexico, and was redesignated as the 49th Tactical Fighter Wing. The move to a larger base with family housing and less vigilant security reduced the cost of operating the unit (in particular, it eliminated the weekly shuttle flights) but it underlined the fact that the F-117's elite status had been eroded.

Since 1991, there have been a few important upgrades to the F-117. Starting in that year, operational aircraft undergoing regular maintenance were upgraded under the Operational Capability Improvement Program

The F-117 has an effectively unlimited range with inflight refueling. A small light behind the cockpit illuminates the refueling receptacle for night operations. *Lockheed*

(OCIP). The first aircraft modified were those that had never gone through WSCS. The principal changes in OCIP involve the cockpit displays; the side displays are replaced by full-color screens and the main IRADS display is replaced by a digital screen, which can show symbology and map data as well as imagery.

The OCIP aircraft also has a Harris digital map system, and a four-dimensional flight management system. This means that the aircraft's automated navigation system can be programmed to arrive over the target at an exact time, and it will manage the airplane's speed en route to do so. Another element of OCIP is a Pilot Activated Automatic Recovery System (PAARS), designed and developed after the 1986 accident, which restores the aircraft to wings-level, gently climbing flight in response to a single switch action. OCIP was completed in early 1994.

From 1994 onward, the fleet was fitted with improved IRADS turrets, which employed focal plane array (FPA) infrared detectors. The solid-state FPAs are more reliable than the old mechanically scanned system and can image targets at a greater distance. Combined with a more powerful laser, this permitted the F-117 to bomb from higher altitudes.

In the late 1990s, the F-117s went through the Ring Laser Gyro Navigation Improvement Program Plus (RNIP+) upgrade, in which the original inertial navigation system was replaced by an RLG inertial platform and a GPS receiver. The RNIP+ system is more accurate and requires far less maintenance and less alignment time, and the GPS provides an independent check on its performance.

Another improvement is the use of the standard Air Force Mission Support System (AFMSS) in place of the original "Elvira." This will allow the F-117s to deploy without C-5s, which were needed to carry the large vans that accommodated the earlier system. The AFMSS was tested at Holloman AFB in 1997.

The next stage is a group of modifications referred to as the F-117 Mid-Life Update (MLU), which includes two main components. Under the Block Cycle 1 program, the aircraft will be fitted with a modernized stores management system that incorporates the MIL-STD-1760 data-bus. Together with the RNIP+, this will make the F-117 compatible with modern weapons such as the Joint Stand-Off Weapon (JSOW) and Joint Direct Attack Munition (JDAM), which are initialized before launch with the GPS coordinates of the target. This will give the F-117 the ability to attack known targets in the face of bad weather or obscurants. Laser-guided weapons will still be used in good weather, because they are more accurate.

The other element of MLU is the Single Configuration Fleet (SCF) program, under which the RAM and RAS on the USAF's F-117s will be standardized. In the original design of the F-117, stealth was given top priority, well ahead of maintenance. The designers minimized the number of quick-access panels, using them only for systems that had to be checked routinely before every flight. Otherwise, the skin is sealed with RAM. To reach most of the avionics, for example, the RAM covering the facet where the access panel is located has to be scraped off and replaced, a process that takes one to two hours, depending on the size of the panel.

The people who do this are known as Material Application and Repair Specialists (MARS). They are nicknamed "Martians" and have adopted the cartoon character Marvin the Martian as their unofficial mascot. To make the Martians' life more interesting, the 59 production F-117s were delivered in several different configurations, with slightly different types of RAM. The largest change was a switch from a sheet material to a sprayed-on RAM. However, all repairs are made with sheet material, so each F-117 has a different patchwork of original, sprayed, and repair material on its surface.

The other major stealth-related maintenance item on the F-117 is the exhaust system, which has been a source of problems since the start of the program and has been under almost continuous development. The exhaust is a metallic structure, covered with non-load-bearing ceramic "bricks" made of a material similar to the tiles used on the exterior of the Space Shuttle. In the original design, the bricks were cemented in place individually, and the seams between them had to be filled with a heat-resistant puttylike material. If the gaps were not properly sealed, hot air could impinge on the metal substructure and cause a fire. Scheduled exhaust maintenance could take 600 manhours, spread over 14 days.

Under the SCF, the RAM will be removed from all aircraft. Next, a number of new quick-access panels will be added, providing easier access to frequently serviced components. The RAM will be replaced by a new sprayed-on coating. This will be more weather-resistant than the sheet

The F-117A has one-piece fast-opening weapon bay doors. The weapons themselves are carried on a trapeze that extends them clear of the weapon bay before they separate from the aircraft. This aircraft is being fit-checked with the new AGM-158A JASSM stand-off missile. *Lockheed*

RAM, which tends to bubble under intense sunlight. The edges of the access panels will be covered by "zip strips," specially developed strips of RAM that can be quickly pulled off the aircraft while leaving the rest of the surface untouched. When the panel is replaced, new zip strips can be installed to fill the gap. The USAF is also looking for a hand-held or robotic spraying tool for making small RAM repairs on the flight-line.

The original exhaust systems have now been replaced by an improved design, which uses a more durable material and interlocking tiles, which require much less sealing. Overall, the goal is to reduce stealth-related maintenance costs by 50 percent.

Another change rectifies what might seem to be a remarkable omission. Until the end of the 1990s, the F-117's maintainers had no direct way to determine whether an F-117's LO systems were working properly or not. Instead, they maintained the RAM and RAS within tight physical limits, carried out close and time-consuming visual inspections, and did not dispatch an aircraft unless it was perfect. Now, the 49th has a

"diagnostic imaging radar" developed by System Planning Corporation. This will allow maintainers to check the stealth characteristics of the F-117 on the flight line.

As the F-117 production line neared its end, Lockheed made the first of many proposals to develop substantially improved versions of the aircraft. After the Navy's A-12 Avenger II project was canceled in 1991, the Skunk Works offered the Pentagon a radically modified aircraft, the A/F-117X, which would be produced in carrier-based and land-based versions. The company even received clearance to brief the British Royal Air Force on the program.

continued on page 68

Right
The F-117 still requires more maintenance than conventional fighters. However, efforts are under way to improve the airplane's surface coatings and exhaust. *Lockheed*

Dual weapon bays, on each side of the central structural keel, can each accommodate a 2,000-pound-class weapon—a substantial internal bomb load for any tactical fighter. *Lockheed*

To this day, F-117 serial numbers break the rules; 816 is the 32nd production aircraft and the 37th in the sequence that started with 780. It was delivered in 1985, not ordered in that year as the markings would suggest. *Lockheed*

In the early 1990s, Lockheed Martin proposed a series of radically improved F-117 derivatives for both the Air Force and Navy. Major changes included a new wing, with greater span and reduced sweep, and a nearly 100 percent boost in power, with a switch to augmented F414 engines. *Lockheed*

Continued from page 64

There had been British involvement in the F-117 program from its earliest days. Observers were somewhat surprised when a Desert Storm–era photo showed an F-117 with RAF Squadron Leader Graham Wardell's name on the canopy sill, but in fact there had been U.K. pilots on the program before its existence was declassified. It was not the first example of Anglo-American cooperation in sensitive programs and, as in other cases, British access was probably not granted freely but was an exchange for technical or operational support. In the same way, the United Kingdom was the only foreign nation to be offered the F-117.

The ultimate A/F-117X retained only the fuselage shape of the original F-117. New wings, with less sweep and greater span, were added, along with separate trapezoidal horizontal tails. The F404 engine was replaced by the more powerful F414, with limited afterburning and new exhausts. The weapon bays would be modified to accommodate much larger loads, and the fighter would have a conventional canopy and a radar. Much of the technology would have been drawn from the F-22 fighter. However, the new aircraft would have been similar enough to the F-117 for Lockheed to produce technology demonstrators by modifying some of the existing F-117As.

Whatever its merits, the proposal's timing was poor. It competed for diminishing defense funds with the F-22 and the successors to the A-12, which the USAF and Navy respectively considered to be more important. The new Clinton administration was anxious to save money and eliminate new fighter programs, rather than add another one, particularly a single-mission attack aircraft. The project remained what Ben Rich liked to call a UFO—an "Un-Funded Opportunity."

Making the F-117 carrier-compatible would have been no trivial task; the new wing would have been fitted with full-span slats and wing spoilers. The Navy was unconvinced. *Lockheed*

In March 1999, the F-117 went to war again, in support of Operation Allied Force, the air campaign against Serbia and its forces in Kosovo. As in Desert Storm, stealth aircraft—a squadron of F-117s deployed from Holloman and B-2s flying direct from Whiteman AFB—were assigned to the most heavily defended targets. Three days after the start of operations, on March 27, an F-117 was shot down over Serbia. With the aid of a massive effort by army special-operations forces, the pilot was recovered safely seven hours after the shoot-down.

The loss of the F-117 has been attributed to a number of factors, including luck. However, the Serbian forces were probably aware of the time at which the F-117 took off from Aviano AB, Italy, and could warn the defenders around likely targets. There have been suggestions that the USAF did not have jamming and support aircraft in the area where the F-117 was hit, and that the F-117s had been repeating the same tactical pattern on successive missions. Although the final shoot-down report is classified, the aircraft was apparently hit by a missile that had been cued on the target by some other asset—whether an early-warning radar whose operators knew where to search, a ground observer, or a fighter pilot. A report in the *New York Times* later said that the shoot-down had been blamed in part on poor missions planning.

Today, the remaining 51 F-117s continue to operate from Holloman and are undergoing SCF modifications as they pass through major depot maintenance at Palmdale. There is no firm retirement date, but they are among the aircraft due to be replaced by the Joint Strike Fighter (JSF) after 2010. They remain the world's largest operational fleet of stealth aircraft—something that would have amazed the planners of the early 1980s. But time, politics, and budgets do not respect plans.

Another change in the so-called A/F-117X was a recontoured underbody, which would double the internal weapons load. It would also have had a more conventional canopy, which—like other parts of the aircraft—would have used F-22 technology. *Lockheed*

Chapter 5

THE 1980s
DREAM PROJECTS

Imagine that today the United States has more than 800 stealth aircraft in service. The number includes 130-plus strategic bombers and two wings of fully operational supersonic fighters, with two more working up. Half the Navy's carrier air wings include attack squadrons with long-range, heavy-payload stealth attack aircraft. More than 150 stealthy fighters and strike aircraft are being delivered every year. Moreover, the USAF's B-1s and B-52s are armed with long-range stealth cruise missiles that no adversary knows how to detect.

It would be good if it were true. Indeed, the Pentagon planned and expected, in 1985, to field such a force by the end of the century. The reasons why it did not happen include technical overreach, gigantic geopolitical changes, and a few very poor decisions.

The first results from the Have Blue pole-model tests made it clear that stealth would be valuable for any military aircraft. From the outset, Have Blue and the follow-on ATA were seen as paving the way for a wide range of stealth warplanes. With this in mind, DARPA and other Pentagon managers were keen to ensure that stealth would not be a monopoly.

In December 1976, months after DARPA awarded the Have Blue flight demonstration contract to Lockheed, the agency invited Northrop to bid on a second and more ambitious demonstration program. One of DARPA's key projects was called Assault Breaker. Its goal was to stop a Soviet tank attack in Central Europe with a hail of precision-guided weapons aimed at the "second echelon"—concentrated masses of armor moving to reinforce the front. It depended on an airborne radar to track the tanks and the incoming missiles. This begged a serious question: how would a radar-carrying airplane survive within line-of-sight of its targets?

The answer was what DARPA called BSAX, for Battlefield Surveillance Aircraft—Experimental, a stealth aircraft carrying a radar, and DARPA planned to give it to Northrop. This would keep Northrop's stealth technology moving and would avoid the risk of distracting Lockheed from Have Blue.

BSAX was more difficult than Have Blue, in several respects. It involved the development of a side-looking LPI radar. Another challenge was that while Have Blue was designed as an attack aircraft, intended to make a straight run for its target and to spend as little time in a defended area as possible, BSAX would have to loiter over the battlefield for hours,

The spectacular full-scale mockup of the McDonnell Douglas/General Dynamics A-12 Avenger II carrier-based bomber. The A-12 had a maximum launch weight of 80,000 pounds and carried both defensive and offensive armament. *Lockheed Martin*

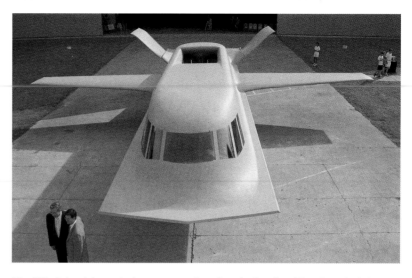

Eleven years after the single Northrop Tacit Blue prototype made its last test flight, the Air Force officially disclosed the existence of the long-rumored "Shamu." It turned out that other companies' engineers had given it that name. To its builders, it was simply known as "the Whale." *Bill Sweetman*

The Whale's wide cockpit accommodated a single pilot. The dorsal air intake for the two Garrett AiResearch ATF3 engines was entirely flush with the upper fuselage, which was good from the RCS viewpoint but bad for pressure recovery. The flared ends of the V-tails were considered necessary for low RCS, although the later YF-23 had straight surfaces. *Bill Sweetman*

during which time it would be illuminated by many radars from different directions. Unlike Have Blue, which was more detectable from the side than from the front and rear, BSAX would have to be the first "all-aspect stealth" design.

Northrop put the first BSAX models on the pole in the summer of 1977. "It was a disaster," says designer Irv Waaland, who was summoned to rescue the program. It was Fred Oshira, one of the electromagneticists who worked for Northrop's stealth guru, John Cashen, who saved Northrop's face—along with other parts of the company's anatomy. "I don't want it to come out this way," muses Cashen, "but Fred could see the waves on the surface of the airplane. He had so much experience in electromagnetics." With the BSAX problems constantly in his mind, Oshira had taken to carrying a piece of modeling clay at all times—even when he took his family to Disneyland. Sitting on a bench, watching his children on the teacup ride, Oshira molded the clay into a new shape, with a rounded top and flat sloped sides that flared down and outward into a knife-edge.

It worked like a charm, flowing the radar energy around the body rather than scattering it like a mirror. Northrop had not only found a way to remain stealthy from any direction, but had significantly expanded the range of radar frequencies that stealth technology could defeat. Northrop's philosophy was inherently compatible with curvature, promising greater aerodynamic efficiency.

With the major RCS problem solved, the BSAX design came together in the second half of 1977. It had a bluff-nosed, bulky body to accommodate the radar. The engines were buried at the rear behind a flush dorsal inlet, with

no screens or grilles. It had an unswept wing, which used a Clark Y airfoil section that had not been seen since the 1930s—the advantage was that the lower surface was flat. Pitch and yaw were controlled by a fly-by-wire system driving two all-moving V-tails. Worried about how the ends of the angled tail would appear on radar, the designers curved the tips of the V-tails toward the horizon. It was a final, organic touch to an already strange design, which soon acquired the nickname Whale. Its official code-name was Tacit Blue.

The Whale flew in 1982 and was tested successfully. Even the LPI radar worked, and designs were in place for a larger production version. What did not work was the radar-controlled missile that Tacit Blue was supposed to guide. The Pentagon decided to use different weapons that did not require terminal guidance—just target location, which could be provided by a larger radar standing off at a greater distance, and carried on a modified Boeing 707. (This is today's Joint STARS radar.) In 1985, Tacit Blue was abruptly canceled and the prototype was stored at Groom Lake. Eleven years later, its existence was declassified and it was moved to the Air Force Museum at Wright-Patterson AFB.

Tacit Blue placed Northrop in contention to develop the USAF's next stealth aircraft—a strategic bomber. This project resulted from a combination of two events in the mid-1970s, the cancellation of the original B-1 program, which left the USAF with an open requirement for a bomber, and the breakthrough in stealth technology. The Carter administration secretly authorized the start of work on a stealth strategic bomber in early 1979. The starting point was Lockheed's ATA B airplane, enlarged and refined with more use of curvature on its wings and other surfaces.

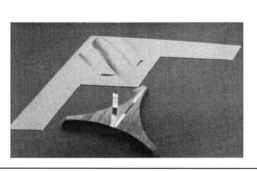

Northrop investigated a number of ways to provide directional control for the B-2. Inward-canted vertical fins were ineffective. After experimenting with tip-mounted fins and reaction jet controls, Northrop settled on a design using split brake-rudders and differential thrust. *Northrop*

The USAF was not content with a Lockheed monopoly on a project as large and important as the new bomber. In the summer of 1979, senior USAF officers pressured Northrop into joining the program, while warning the company that its work was an "insurance policy" against problems with Lockheed's aircraft.

The two companies approached the problem from different directions. Although Lockheed's design has never been declassified, most descriptions suggest that it never diverged completely from its roots in Have Blue. Northrop started with a clean sheet of paper and an analysis of the threat, and its first design was a high-altitude, efficient flying wing. As the designs matured—and as the USAF expanded the specification, calling for a heavier weapon load and the ability to penetrate air defenses at both high and low altitude—the Northrop design's advantage over Lockheed increased. By September 1980, when the USAF issued a request for proposals (RFP) for the Advanced Technology Bomber, Northrop had advanced to near-equal status in the competition. When the contract was awarded in October 1981, Northrop was the winner.

The plan was to fly the first B-2 bomber in late 1987. By that time, the bomber would be in production. By 1991 or 1992, the first squadron would be operational and Northrop and its partners (Boeing and Vought) would be building 30 bombers a year.

Development was more complex than expected. Not only was the bomber large and stealthy—with better capability against low-frequency radars and across all aspects than the F-117—but it was the first military aircraft of any size to be built primarily from composite materials. Northrop's "seamless" shaping technique was intolerant of gaps, steps, or geometrical errors, so the bomber had to be built with unprecedented precision. The only way to do this was to use a computer-driven system for design, manufacture, and assembly. No such system existed, and it had to be created from scratch. The B-2 carried a complex suite of avionics, including an LPI radar and an electronic warfare system that could detect, locate, and identify threats and compute their detection range against the bomber—both of which were entirely new for a bomber.

The first B-2 was unveiled in November 1988, almost a year after it was supposed to fly, but it was not ready to begin testing; it did not take to the air until July 17 of the following year. Even that date had only been met by slowing work on subsequent aircraft, and the second B-2 did not get airborne until October 1990. By that time, a wary Congress had vetoed any "concurrent" production of the B-2. Production could not start until the aircraft was proven in tests, and it was already clear that the bomber was years away from becoming operational.

Alongside the bomber program was a parallel project to develop a stealth cruise missile. U.S. intelligence had clear indications that the Soviet Union was improving its air defenses in the late 1970s, and that one aim of the improvements was to intercept the then-new Boeing AGM-86 cruise missile. A stealthy cruise missile, flying at low altitude, would be almost impossible to intercept.

The first stealth cruise missile was a Lockheed Skunk Works project code-named Senior Prom. It was tested successfully in 1981–1982, using a C-130 as the launch platform. For unspecified reasons, however, Senior Prom was not put into production. Ben Rich described the weapon as a scaled-down Have Blue shape, without the cockpit, and some reports

One of the challenges in developing the B-2 was the need for great precision in the outer contours of the aircraft. This forced the contractors to develop the first computer-aided design system in which the entire product was defined electronically; there was no B-2 mockup. The computers here look primitive, but were the state of the art in 1985. *Northrop*

Right
The B-2 lifts off for its first flight, on July 17, 1989. By this time, the program was under attack from Congress because of delays and increasing costs, and the Soviet Union—the adversary against which the B-2 had been designed—was losing its grip on Eastern Europe. The Berlin Wall fell five months later. *Northrop*

from the time suggested that the missile was not designed, to be compatible with internal rotary weapon launchers. This would not be entirely surprising, since the B-1 had not been revived as a production program when the weapon was designed and the B-52 was expected to carry cruise missiles externally.

DARPA, in 1982, launched another cruise-missile program called Teal Dawn—with extremely advanced goals. In August of that year, in Monterey, California, a DARPA program manager, U.S. Navy Commander Donald Finch, substituted for the agency's director as the keynote speaker for the Association for Unmanned Vehicle Systems annual convention. Seldom has a substitute made such a strong impression, as Commander Finch outlined DARPA's plan for the next generation of cruise missiles.

By the 1990s, said Finch, the United States could field cruise missiles smaller than the 3,000-pound AGM-86 but with near-global range—almost 7,000 miles. They would have autonomous guidance systems, be accurate enough to threaten most targets without nuclear warheads, and would be able to detect and respond to threats in flight. They would also be stealthy. "There are not enough rubles to defend against something like this," said Finch.

This extraordinary weapon would be made possible through new technologies and subsystems designed for the cruise-missile mission, said Finch, who pointed out that the then-new AGM-86 and Tomahawk were based on existing aircraft technology. The intercontinental missile would take advantage of a new fuel, with twice as much energy per pound as normal jet fuel. It would have a regenerative engine cycle that could recover waste exhaust heat and recycle it into the compressor, reducing fuel consumption and

greatly diminishing its infrared signature. Such an engine was under study by Williams International, producer of the AGM-86 engine. Another radical engine was studied by Garrett, combining turbine and diesel features.

The USAF's only operational intercontinental cruise missile was called the Snark, after a mythical beast in a poem by Lewis Carroll. DARPA's project ought to have been called the Boojum, after another creature in the same poem, because—like anyone unfortunate enough to meet Carroll's Boojum—it softly and suddenly vanished away, and never was heard of again.

The most likely explanation for the project's disappearance, in those early Reagan/Weinberger years, is that it was considered sufficiently threatening (both to the Soviet Union and the U.S. strategic weapons establishment) to be designated as a black program. Because it was unaffected by strategic-arms treaties—which applied only to air-launched cruise missiles—it also offered the United States a chance to break out of these limits.

How far it proceeded is anyone's guess. Elements of the project may have reemerged in the form of the long-range conventional strike weapon (LRCSW) project of the late 1980s, which used a high-speed propeller to provide a modest advance in cruise missile performance, or in the scene-matching guidance system used in later Tomahawk variants.

Meanwhile, General Dynamics won a contract in 1983 to develop a rather more conventional stealthy cruise missile, the AGM-129 Advanced Cruise Missile (ACM). The ACM was an interesting example of the use of

A view of the B-2 on its first take-off shows its extraordinary, almost organic, shape. The wing leading edge is particularly strange at first sight, but it represents a compromise between aerodynamics, which require a rounded edge, and signatures, which drive the designers to sharp edges. The leading edges have a toothpick profile, sharp at the ends and rounded in the middle. *Northrop*

shaping to meet a very specific mission requirement. The missile's body had a constant section over most of its length, with straight sides. The nose was pyramidal and faceted. The Williams F112 engine was fed by a flush inlet under the body, and the exhaust was RAM-treated and concealed by a beaver tail. The wings were swept forward and "radome-structured" as were the tail surfaces.

From head-on and above—the low-flying missile would not be seen from below—the nose and wings were swept away from the radar. The inlet and exhaust were shielded by the body. From the side, the ACM's straight body sides would cause a distinct spike, but it did not matter. The only way that an airborne radar could detect the low-flying missile against ground clutter would be to use Doppler processing, which depended on the difference in velocity of the target and the ground, relative to the radar. If the radar was at right angles to the ACM, there would be no such difference; the Doppler shifts in the target and ground returns would be the same.

The ACM entered service in 1990, but strategic weapons cutbacks reduced production to 460 missiles, deployed on B-52H bombers.

After Senior Prom, the next stealth project in which the Skunk Works became involved was its most unusual. Teamed with Lockheed Missiles and Space Company in Sunnyvale, California, the Skunks built a ship. Under a contract awarded in October 1982, Lockheed built a 563-ton, 164-foot-long research vessel called *Sea Shadow*. The ship was delivered in March 1985, and stole secretly out of San Francisco Bay on a series of classified tests, concealed by a specially built barge.

Sea Shadow looked nothing like a ship. A faceted superstructure with sloping sides, resembling a black barn roof, perched on top of two slender submarine-like hulls. The twin-hull design minimized the ship's wake. (A British naval stealth expert, remarking on the low-RCS design of the Soviet cruiser *Kirov*, once remarked that "if you saw a huge wake on radar with nothing in front of it, you knew you'd found *Kirov*.") Diesel engines in the superstructure, isolated from the water, drove propulsors via electric motors.

Ben Rich would later recall that the program both violated and proved Kelly Johnson's unwritten 15th law of the Skunk Works: "Starve before you do business with the Navy." Lockheed designed an operational version of the

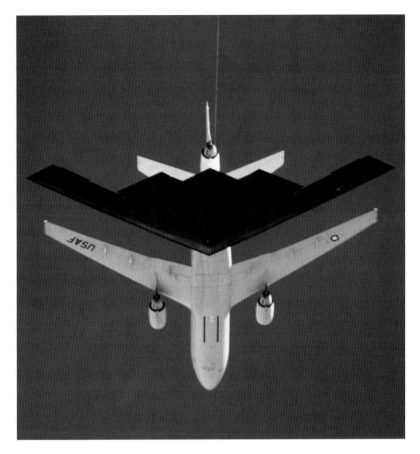

The B-2 measures about the same from nose to tail as an F-15, but its wingspan is slightly greater than that of the Air Force's KC-10 Extender tanker. Gross weight is about the same as that of a Boeing 767 airliner. *Northrop*

Northrop and Lockheed had also briefed the Navy on stealth technology and carrier-based designs based on features of the B-2 and F-117.

The Navy shelved studies for a dual-purpose nonstealthy aircraft, known as VFMX, which would have replaced the Grumman A-6 and F-14, and launched a secret program to develop an Advanced Tactical Aircraft (ATA) using stealth technology. However, the Navy's aircraft-development budget was already overstretched, and the service did not want to place total reliance on a single radical aircraft. To preserve funds, the Navy insisted that the ATA should be developed under a fixed-price contract.

The Navy program managers directed the potential ATA competitors to form teams. Lockheed was teamed with Boeing, Northrop with Grumman and Vought, and McDonnell Douglas with General Dynamics. Lacking any strong experience with carrier-based combat aircraft, the Lockheed-Boeing team was eliminated. In 1984, the Northrop/Grumman and GD/McDonnell Douglas teams were awarded contracts to refine their designs and to demonstrate critical technologies.

The requirement was extremely demanding. ATA was not a relatively small attack aircraft—as fragmentary reports described it—but the largest bomber to be designed for carrier use since the nuclear-capable A-3 and supersonic A-5 Vigilante of the 1950s and 1960s. The Navy wanted a 12,000-pound internal bomb load, plus AGM-88 HARM and AIM-120

The Air Force's original plan was to replace all its B-52s with a force of 100 B-1s and 132 B-2s. Today, there are only 21 B-2s and the B-52H is expected to remain in service until almost 2040. *U.S. Air Force*

Sea Shadow as an air defense picket, armed with Patriot SAMs and cruising 300 miles ahead of the fleet, where any conventional ship would be an isolated target. It would use LPI radar to detect Soviet bombers and intercept them before they could launch their antishipping missiles. But the project was seen as a direct threat to the Navy's Aegis cruisers and destroyers, and the Navy showed little interest in it. *Sea Shadow* was declassified in 1993, but went back to sea in 1999 as a test platform for the Zumwalt-class destroyer—planned as the U.S. Navy's first true stealth ship.

After the loss of the B-2 competition, the Skunk Works spearheaded Lockheed's effort to win the next two major stealth programs, the USAF's Advanced Tactical Fighter, and a stealth bomber for the U.S. Navy. It was successful in the first venture, but not in the second—which was probably just as well, because the project ended in catastrophe.

The Navy was late to the study of stealth aircraft, but in 1983, Navy Secretary John Lehman became convinced that a stealth attack aircraft would be an ideal weapon for the service's new maritime strategy, which called for the Navy's carrier air groups to attack targets in the Northern Soviet Union.

Advanced Medium-Range Air-to-Air Missiles (AMRAAM) missiles for self-defense, and a range of more than 1,000 miles.

Northrop and Grumman responded with an aircraft that strongly resembled a scaled-down version of the original B-2 design, with a single-notch trailing-edge design. The McDonnell Douglas/GD design was based on early stealth work by General Dynamics, including an early tailless project (known as Sneaky Pete) and a LO aircraft that had been studied by the USAF during the early days of the ATF program. It was a pure triangle with a leading-edge sweepback of 48 degrees and no tail surfaces. The layout combined a long wing span—for low approach speeds—with a great deal of internal volume, and the aircraft was very compact when the outer wings were folded.

The competition was not decided on the merits of the designs. Northrop and Grumman, which between them had built all-weather carrier-based attack airplanes and stealth aircraft, considered that the ATA could not be developed for a fixed price and refused to bid on such terms. The Navy considered their bid "nonresponsive." McDonnell Douglas and GD, with less experience, agreed to a fixed-price bid and were awarded a full-scale development contract in early 1988. The goal was to fly the first aircraft in 1990 and reach full-rate production in 1994. In 1989, the bomber was named Avenger II—expropriating an old Grumman name in a blatant pitch to President George Bush, who had flown a TBF Avenger in World War II.

One factor that played a part in the companies' decision to accept a fixed-price contract was that the potential payoff was massive. The U.S. Navy planned to put two squadrons of A-12s on each carrier. (Its radar had an air-to-air mode and it would have been able to carry the long-range AIM-155 Advanced AAM, the replacement for the F-14's Phoenix, so it would have played an important role in air defense as well as attack.) Including some aircraft for the U.S. Marine Corps, the Navy stated a total requirement for

The B-2 is unique in its ability to carry large weapons internally. Here, the bomber releases a GBU-37—a 4,700-pound hard-target weapon equipped with GPS guidance. *Northrop*

Northrop's answer to the problem of a stealthy air data system was to use sets of four flush ports (one for each channel of the quadruplex fly-by-wire system) located around the center-section leading edge of the wing. *Bill Sweetman*

Flow visualization: A B-2 on a low-altitude, high-speed test flight gives a dramatic demonstration of the unusual air velocity patterns over its wing and inlets. *Northrop*

858 aircraft. Moreover, under a 1985 agreement, the USAF had designated the A-12 as the replacement for the F-111 and the F-15E attack aircraft, and the Navy nominated an ATF variant as the follow-on to the F-14. The USAF requirement would take production of the A-12 to more than 1,200 aircraft.

The A-12's technology was not quite as advanced as that of the ATF, in some key areas, with modest maneuverability requirements. Its engine, the General Electric F412-GE-400, was an advanced derivative of the F/A-18's F404 with a larger fan and no afterburner. Rather than using new active-array radar technology, its Norden Systems APQ-183 attack radar had a single power source and dual passive electronically scanned arrays. The radar installation resembled that of the B-2, with the antennas embedded in the leading edge of the wing.

In other respects, though, the design was ambitious. With a gross weight as high as 80,000 pounds, it was more like a mini-B-2 than an A-6 replacement. The airframe was largely made of composite material. Meeting carrier-landing requirements with a tailless aircraft was no easy task. As well as having full-span trailing-edge flaps and leading-edge flaps on the outer wings, the A-12 had a "pitch flap" above the coupled exhaust nozzle to provide a measure of vectored thrust.

The A-12 reflected a philosophy of stealth design that had been developed at General Dynamics, and was subtly but significantly different from the Lockheed and Northrop approaches. GD's approach did not depend on stealth alone, but stealth in combination with situational awareness, tactics, and self-defense. As well as featuring an LO design and radar-absorbent edge structures (supplied by Rockwell's Tulsa division), the A-12 had an advanced Litton Amecom ALD-11 electronic surveillance measures (ESM) suite that could detect and identify emitters and locate them accurately. It also had an infrared search and track (IRST) system for passive detection of airborne targets, and a terrain-following system, based on a digital map, which permitted all-weather low-level flight without causing radar emissions. One small but significant feature of the A-12 was its cockpit canopy, which was quite conventional (not frameless like that of the ATF) and provided both crew members with good visibility.

GD's philosophy was that no feasible level of stealth would totally prevent radars from illuminating the target. With the ALD-11, however, the crew could detect emitters and pick their way through the gaps in the radar chain that were opened up by reduced RCS. If there was no alternative to flying within detection range of a radar, there was always a brace of HARMs on board. Moreover, the Navy was also developing a small inertially guided gliding cluster bomb, the Advanced Interdiction Weapon System (AIWS), which the A-12 could launch at an emitter detected by the ALD-11. An incoming A-12 could launch a HARM to suppress a threatening radar and force it to shut down, then kill it with an AIWS so it would not bother following aircraft—and still carry 11,000 pounds of ordnance to the target. Hostile fighters could be detected by the IRST or the APQ-183 (which had an unusually large field of view, militating against surprise attacks) and engaged with the AIM-120.

However, the program soon hit major problems. Some of these concerned stealth technology, but the overriding difficulty was weight. The combination of an all-wing layout, carrier operations, and composite materials had taken the designers into unknown territory. An all-wing

Despite maintenance challenges, the Air Force was able to deploy five B-2s to Guam in March 1998. A year later, the bomber performed its first combat sorties over Kosovo. *U.S Air Force*

Left

B-2 production stopped at 21 aircraft; but as this book closes for press, Northrop Grumman is preparing plans to build 40 more aircraft, in response to the Bush administration's interest in long-range airpower. *Northrop*

Right top

General Dynamics (now Raytheon) was responsible for the design of the AGM-129 Advanced Cruise Missile (ACM). Equipped with forward-swept wings, which folded out from under a panel on the upper side of the body, the nuclear-armed ACM was powered by a Williams F112 engine. *Omaha World-Herald*

Right

The ACM's straight sides were an ideal stealth solution for a low-flying object, making it an almost impossible target for an airborne Doppler radar. *Omaha World-Herald*

Below

The A-12's F412 engines were installed on either side of the centerline. Outboard of each engine was a massive weapon bay, the two bays accommodating a total of 12,000 pounds of internal ordnance. Defensive weapon bays, outboard of the main landing gear wells, each held an AGM-88 HARM and an AIM-120 AMRAAM. *Lockheed Martin*

aircraft is efficient because its mass is evenly distributed across the wing span, but the impact of a carrier landing, or the stress imposed by a catapult launch or arrested recovery, drives large point loads through the landing gear and tailhook attachments. One specific problem concerned the lower wing skins. The designers had started with light, thin skins to handle flight loads, but it turned out that the most difficult case was a hard carrier landing with a full reserve fuel load. The wings and fuel tanks were much deeper than those of any other Navy aircraft, and the weight of the fuel put an unexpectedly heavy load on the wing skins. They had to be made thicker and heavier.

By 1990, the Navy program managers thought that, at best, the A-12 would be 7,900 pounds above its initial design empty weight when it entered service—a massive 25 per cent overrun. On the other hand, improvements in other areas, combined with some early conservatism in initial estimates, meant that the A-12's performance in many key areas, including mission radius, met either the specification or the Navy's estimates. But the Navy managers exacerbated the problem by telling the manufacturers to fix the problems within the fixed price and the existing schedule while concealing the problems from their superiors. In early 1990, Defense Secretary Dick Cheney assured Congress that all was well with the project.

Cheney's comments were in support of the Pentagon's first substantial review of its aircraft programs since the removal of the Berlin Wall in 1989. The Major Aircraft Review, published in March 1990, reflected not only the realization that the threat of war was receding but the recognition that spending plans were becoming unaffordable. The new stealth aircraft were all costing more and taking longer than expected to develop, and the cost of each airplane was now expected to exceed the initial, optimistic projections. Under the review, all of them were trimmed back and production was stretched out. The USAF's B-2 force was cut from 132 to 75 aircraft, and the peak production rate was cut from 30 to 12 aircraft per year. The ATF buy was reduced from 750 to 648 aircraft at a top rate of 48 aircraft a year. The Navy's A-12 buy was reduced to 620 aircraft at 48 per year.

Late in 1990, Cheney discovered the extent of the A-12's problems and, infuriated, canceled the project in January 1991. However, this did not help the other stealth programs. In the aftermath of the cancellation, the Navy launched a study for a replacement aircraft, the A-X, but diverted most of its resources to an enlarged version of the F/A-18, the Super Hornet.

During 1991, B-2 testing revealed unexpected stealth problems. The program was already experiencing cost overruns and delays due to difficulties with its radar, its defensive electronics, and other features, and it was becoming increasingly clear that flight tests would continue into 1997. The USAF and Northrop devised a three-stage block upgrade program, culminating in a fully operational aircraft, but Congress was skeptical and reluctant to authorize more than the 16 production aircraft (plus 5 development aircraft) that were under contract by 1991.

In January 1992, as one of a number of cutbacks in strategic weapon programs, President Bush announced that the administration would not attempt to acquire more than 16 production B-2s. At that time, conventional wisdom held that Bush would be easily elected to a second term in the elections of November 1992. But this did not happen, and President Clinton's first secretary of defense, Les Aspin, was a long-standing critic of the B-2. Aspin was a supporter of the idea that stealth aircraft should be "silver bullets" used in small numbers to open the way for a larger force of conventional aircraft. Despite numerous studies and proposals, no further B-2 production was authorized, and the program entered a protracted deployment phase.

The F-22 was also delayed, as recounted in the next chapter; and neither the Navy's A-X nor the joint-service A/F-X that followed it proceeded beyond the study phase. By 2000, the United States had only 70 stealth aircraft in service and was building only a handful of F-22s, a far cry from the plans of 1985.

There were three key factors behind the change. The end of the Cold War robbed the stealth program of its urgency. The Clinton administration wanted to curb military spending, but it presided over an economic boom that forced the services to spend money on wages rather than materiel, so projects were stretched, deferred, or canceled. Last, it has to be admitted that stealth aircraft cost more than expected.

The B-2 and the A-12 had both overrun their budgets. The A-12 had proven overweight. While the theory of stealth was sound, it had been found in every stealth program that it was the systems that were influenced by stealth, from LPI radars to engine inlets and exhausts, added weight, cost, and time to the program. Moreover, maintaining stealth aircraft in ready-to-go condition was a constant challenge. In later stealth projects, the goal would not be achieving ever-lower levels of detectability—the slow pace of improvement in the threat made that unnecessary—but in making sure that the airplane would be mature and operable when it entered service.

Smooth, gray, broad-bodied, apparently unarmed, and deceptively conventional, the F-22 Raptor represents the greatest single advance in fighter design since the advent of the jet.

The F-22 features stealth, supercruise, and integrated avionics. No other fighter, in service or under development, matches the F-22 in any one of these attributes. No other known aircraft combines any two of them. All three are essential to the way the F-22 flies and fights.

The F-22's F-117-like stealth has two main purposes. By protecting the F-22 against detection and attack from airborne or ground-based weapons, it endows the fighter with much greater freedom of operation. It also gives the pilot a greater chance of achieving surprise in the attack and allows missiles to be launched at closer range.

Supersonic cruise—the F-22 is capable of cruising 50 percent faster than any fighter today, without using full military power—has defensive and offensive value. Combined with stealth, it reduces the fighter's susceptibility to SAMs and other weapons. By the time a SAM radar detects an approaching F-22, the fighter may overfly it before a missile can reach its altitude, turning the engagement into a tail-chase in which the missile quickly runs out of energy. A supercruising fighter is less likely to be surprised by an attacker approaching from its rear quadrant, and more likely to surprise a slower adversary. Higher speeds give the F-22's missiles more energy at launch and, consequently, in the end-game.

The integrated avionics system allows the pilot to exploit stealth and supercruise tactically. The F-22 avionics system fuses the inputs from onboard and offboard sensors, giving the pilot the situational awareness necessary to handle an air combat scenario that unrolls 50 percent faster than it does for the pilot of a subsonic aircraft. The sensors are managed automatically, to maximize the use of off-board and passive sensors and to minimize the chance that the F-22's emissions will be detected.

This capability has not been developed overnight. When the F-22 enters service in late 2005, more than 20 years will have passed since the USAF started committing serious money to the project.

At the start of the 1980s, it was clear that Soviet planners had set out to meet the threat posed by new, agile U.S. fighters in three ways. One was the development of new, fast, agile, and heavily armed fighters, the Mikoyan

The F-22 is basically a clipped-delta design, with twin booms carrying its horizontal tail surfaces. One of the design's most unusual features is that the horizontals intersect the wing trailing edges. Edge alignments are very apparent in this view. *Lockheed Martin*

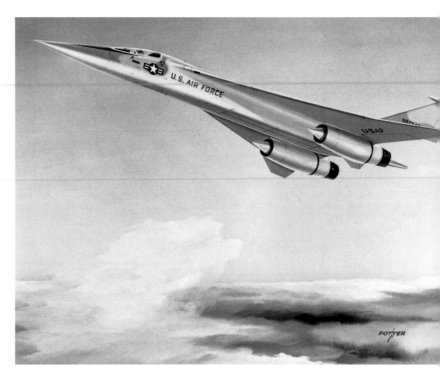

Faster and higher were the watchwords for some manufacturers as they started to look at a replacement for the F-15. This was a Boeing design armed with long-range air-to-surface missiles, with canards and thrust vectoring. *Boeing*

This is another Boeing concept, with fully internal weapon carriage, no canards, and twin vertical tails. By 1982, the company was smarting from its failure to win a leading role on the U.S Air Force's new bomber program and was determined to get back into the fighter business. *Boeing*

MiG-29 and the larger, long-range Sukhoi Su-27. Almost more worrisome was the continued development of improved surface-to-air missiles.

In November 1981, the USAF received Pentagon approval to go ahead with development of an Advanced Tactical Fighter (ATF) and seven companies presented their initial responses to the RFI. The responses were remarkably diverse. Northrop offered a "co-operative fighter" with a gross weight of 17,700 pounds. Lockheed's design was seven times bigger—clearly related to the SR-71, it had a take-off weight of 116,400 pounds and a cruising speed of Mach 2.8. Between these two points lay a spread of configurations including sweptback, swept-forward and unswept wings, and blended deltas.

The USAF selected four concepts for more detailed study: a subsonic stealth aircraft; a Northrop-like low-cost fighter; Lockheed's 50-ton monster; and a supersonic cruise and maneuver (SCM) fighter that fell into the middle of the pack for weight and performance, and would make some use of LO technology. The SCM did best in the air-to-air mission. Cruising above 50,000 feet at speeds of Mach 1.4–1.5, it could evade many SAMs; it was also more maneuverable than the big Lockheed aircraft, but weighed half as much.

With very basic requirements in hand, the USAF was able to estimate the ATF's size and start development of the engines. (Having experienced

growing pains with the F-15's engines, the USAF was determined to begin work on the ATF engines early.) In September 1983, Pratt & Whitney was awarded a contract for its XF119 and General Electric started work on the XF120.

The USAF issued its first request for proposals for what was called the "concept development and investigation" (CDI) stage of the ATF program in May 1983—and amended it significantly eight days later, because of the black art of stealth. The USAF had expected that the ATF would use stealth technology, but security firewalls separated most participants in the ATF program from the highly classified projects under which stealth aircraft such as the F-117, Northrop Tacit Blue, and B-2 were being designed and developed.

The leaders of TAC and USAF Systems Command were aware of these programs, and decided to establish a conduit between the Directorate of Low Observables, buried in Wright-Patterson AFB's locked vaults, and the "white" world of ATF. Then-Major Claude Bolton, leader of the ATF concept development team, has recalled that "someone grabbed us by the shoulder as we walked down the hall and said 'We need to talk to you.'"

Bolton and his colleagues learned that the F-117 and Tacit Blue had demonstrated minuscule RCS numbers, and that designers were developing techniques and materials that promised dramatic RCS reductions without

Lockheed responded to the initial ATF request for information with a design not unlike this one: a high-supersonic, high-altitude aircraft resembling a modernized SR-71. The design reflected fears that the Soviet Union would deploy so many high-performance surface-to-air missiles that the airspace below 50,000 feet would be almost unusable. *Lockheed*

a sharp increase in weight and drag. The ATF RFP was amended, calling for more LO data.

The USAF decided to conduct an extensive "demonstration and validation" (Dem/Val) program with at least two competitors, in which the riskiest technologies would be tested at large scale. The final request for proposals for the Dem/Val program was issued in September 1985. There were still seven fighter design teams in the United States, and all of them responded—Boeing, General Dynamics, Grumman, Lockheed, McDonnell Douglas, Northrop, and Rockwell.

Lockheed's original ATF design echoed the F-117, with an arrowhead planform and a leading-edge "glove" that extended in a straight line to the nose. However, it featured more conventional trapezoidal wings, vectored thrust, and a horizontal tail. The body cross-section resembled an inverted F-117, with the inlets beneath the wing. Internally, it featured a single weapons bay in the midfuselage housing a rotary launcher.

Lockheed and Northrop had gone much farther than any of their rivals in blending stealth with supersonic speed and agility. McDonnell Douglas, in particular, was expected to be a strong contender to replace the F-15, but

General Dynamics' initial response to the Air Force's very broad request was entirely opposite to Lockheed's approach: a subsonic, low-observable design, which became known to the Air Force by the corresponding initials— SLO. It would be the starting point for the A-12 design. *Lockheed Martin*

Left

GD's quest for higher performance and agility in its all-wing designs continued through the mid-1980s. Now part of Lockheed Martin, the Fort Worth team still has a group looking at the challenges of supersonic, tailless aircraft. *Lockheed Martin*

Left

The search for adequate controllability combined with LO led to some remarkably creative solutions, such as the cranked wingtip surfaces on this wind-tunnel model. *Lockheed Martin*

Below

Reverting to a less-blended, more conventional design, GD found itself in trouble combining stability, weight, and LO. In this design, the engineers appear to have given up and grafted the tail of a B-32 Dominator onto the fighter. *Lockheed Martin*

some of its senior executives were convinced that the emphasis on stealth was overrated, and listened instead to F-15 pilots and Tactical Air Command officers, who were more skeptical about the new technology.

Because it was clear that USAF money alone would not support a winning effort, and that contractors would have to invest heavily, five of the competitors formed teams: Boeing and Lockheed with GD, and Northrop with McDonnell Douglas. In October 1986, Lockheed's YF-22 and Northrop's YF-23 were announced as the winners.

Dem/Val was the largest fighter competition in history, lasting more than four years and costing almost $2 billion. Each ATF team built two prototype aircraft. One of each pair of prototypes would have the P&W YF119, and the other would be powered by the GE YF120. The teams would build complete integrated avionics systems, and fly them on test-bed aircraft.

The Lockheed team quickly encountered a snag. The original design would not fly. It could not be controlled in pitch; the pitch-up

Left

In this GD design, the vertical tails have been moved far outboard to clear the vortices from the wing-body junction. The aeroelastic implications would have been interesting, to say the least. *Lockheed Martin*

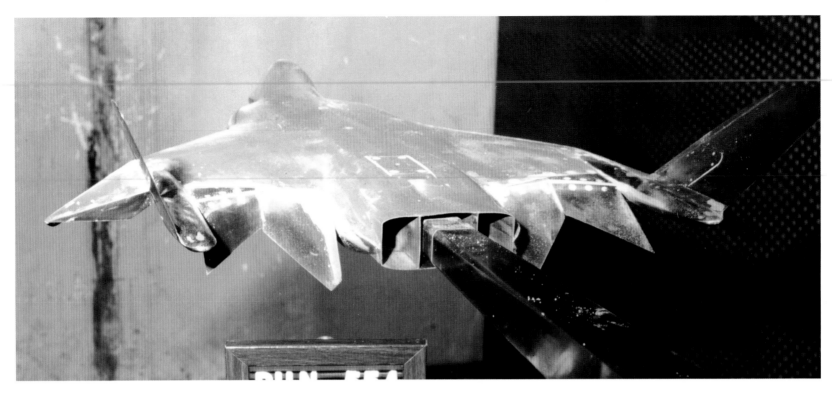

In a near-final design, GD has added a saw-toothed trailing edge to its ATF design, retaining the outboard fins. *Lockheed Martin*

force generated by the glove overwhelmed the force that any reasonable tail surfaces could provide. The team's attempts to fix the original design lasted into the summer of 1987, until it was thrown out in July. It was not until May 1988 that the new design was frozen, with a diamond wing and tails.

When the YF-22 and YF-23 were unveiled, in the summer of 1990, it was clear that the two teams had driven in different directions. Northrop's clipped-diamond wing and V-tails showed that the emphasis was on stealth; Lockheed's vectoring nozzles and more conventional controls revealed a concern for low-speed agility. The first YF-22 flew on September 29, as soon as its YF120 engines were flight-qualified. Both teams flew their second aircraft in late October. A short, intense period of flight-testing followed—the two F-22s made 74 test flights in three months. In early November, the first YF-22 sustained Mach 1.58 without afterburner. During December, it demonstrated its spectacular low-speed maneuverability, performing 360-degree rolls at a 60-degree angle of attack.

Both aircraft met the key requirements, so the decision hinged not just on what the contractors promised in their proposals for engineering and manufacturing development (EMD), but on the customer's confidence in their ability to deliver. In early 1991, as the USAF evaluated the proposals, Northrop's partner, McDonnell Douglas, found itself embroiled in the collapse of the A-12 Avenger, while Lockheed's F-117 became the hero of the Gulf War. Together with the F-22's greater dogfighting potential, these considerations carried the day, and Lockheed was announced the winner of the EMD contract in April 1991. Pratt & Whitney's F119 was chosen as the ATF powerplant.

The F-22 schedule has slipped since the contract was awarded in August 1991. Technical problems have little to do with this very deliberate pace. Development has been a success story. The engine passed its Critical Design Review (CDR) in 1992, and the aircraft did the same in February 1995. Problems such as weight gains, RCS snags, and a shortfall in engine efficiency did occur, but they were discovered well before the first flight and were resolved without delaying the program.

Money has been a different matter. Budget cuts have delayed initial operating capability from 2001 to 2005. The Pentagon has reduced the planned F-22 fleet twice—from 648 to 442 aircraft, in the 1993 "bottom-up review" of U.S. defense plans, and then down to 339 in the mid-1997 Quadrennial Defense Review. The last review also cut the peak production rate from 48 to 36 aircraft a year. However, the USAF still regards the project that is under way today as its highest priority. The F-22 team has created a fighter of deceptively conservative appearance but with remarkable performance.

The F-22's shape is dictated by the requirements of stealth, supersonic cruise, and agility. Stealth demands that all weapons and fuel be carried internally, and this influences the shape and angle of all external surfaces.

Ultimately, GD could not close its design with the outboard verticals, and had to revert to a large single tail. This had deleterious effects on the side-on RCS numbers and helped push GD into third place in the final selection. *Lockheed Martin*

Below

Lockheed won one of the two ATF demonstration/validation contracts with this design. It was overweight and could not be controlled in pitch, but fortunately for Lockheed, these awkward facts did not emerge until after the contract was awarded. *Lockheed Martin*

McDonnell Douglas' ATF program manager was convinced that the Air Force's emphasis on stealth was a passing fad, and that the service really wanted an improved F-15. The company's final design proved unappealing. *Boeing*

Left
Rockwell International entered the ATF contest with a stealthier version of this heavily blended, almost-all-wing design. *Rockwell*

Supersonic cruise requires low supersonic drag, which means a relatively high wing sweep and thin sections for the wing and tail surfaces. Agility is achieved through a large wing span and area and effective controls.

The F-22 is a large airplane, bigger in all directions than the F-15, with a broad body and large internal fuel capacity. The F-22 bucks the trend toward composites; only 25 percent of the airframe weight is composite, and 41 percent is titanium. The wing is a large-area clipped delta—efficient at high speeds, light in weight, and with plenty of fuel volume. The wing is more sophisticated than it looks; large leading-edge flaps and complex camber make it more efficient at low speed and high alpha than earlier deltas.

The F-22 was designed to be able to reach extreme angles of attack while remaining under full control, and to recover safely from high alpha

This artist's concept may represent Grumman's ATF design. The company had not built an Air Force fighter (or any other Air Force aircraft, for that matter) since 1940 and never stood a chance. *Grumman*

even without the help of its thrust-vectoring exhaust nozzles. The wing is located well aft, and the horizontal stabilizers are so close to it that the trailing-edge flaps are cut away to accommodate their leading edges. The surfaces work together for pitch and differentially for roll. When the nozzles are operating, they provide most of the pitch authority, and the tails are primarily used to roll the aircraft.

The maximum speed—between Mach 1.8 and Mach 2.0—is lower than the nominal maximum speed of the F-15. But the F-15 can attain its top speed only with a minimal weapons load and no external fuel, and most pilots never see 2.5 on the Machmeter. The F-22 has plenty of thrust for Mach 2.5—but providing that performance would have demanded variable inlets and higher-temperature materials throughout the aircraft.

The principal breakthrough in terms of straight-line performance is supercruise. The USAF has stated that "about 30 minutes in a one-hour mission" can be flown at supersonic speed, three to six times the supersonic

endurance of any fighter using augmentors. On a typical mission, the F-22 can sustain supersonic speed for most of the time that it is over hostile territory—30 minutes at Mach 1.5 is equivalent to more than 250 miles each way. Supersonic endurance varies with speed. A supercruising F-22 may vary its speed between Mach 1.1–1.2 to Mach 1.5-plus, according to the tactical situation.

Supercruise goes along with high altitude. USAF fighters are normally limited to a maximum altitude of 50,000 feet because, if power and cockpit pressure are lost, the pilot will lose consciousness before the aircraft descends into thicker air. The F-22 life-support ensemble has been chamber-tested to 66,000 feet, and its emergency oxygen system will function long enough for the pilot to reach lower altitudes.

The F-22 should be able to match the agility of any other aircraft in service or under development. Its flight envelope is very large. Alphas as high as 60 degrees have been demonstrated, and some roll maneuverability is retained at that extreme pitch angle. At alphas of 15 degrees and above, the F-22 rolls at least twice as fast as the F-15, and the gap widens until the F-15 hits its roll limit of 30 degrees alpha.

The F-22 will be able to get around its envelope quickly. Maximum pitch rates, boosted by vectored thrust, are up to twice as fast as the F-16. In fact, the F-22's pitch rate is so fast that it is inhibited by a soft stop in the aft movement of the sidestick. The stop is there to remind the pilot that the F-22 is about to respond very fast and that the smart anti-g valve will respond in turn. Lockheed Martin engineers and pilots have named the maximum pitch-rate regime "Mongo mode" in tribute to the horse-punching heavy from the movie *Blazing Saddles*.

One reason such a large aircraft is so fast and agile is that the Pratt & Whitney F119-PW-100 is the most powerful fighter engine ever designed, with a maximum augmented thrust of 39,000 pounds—giving the F-22 more power than two F-4s. Even so, maximum thrust does not tell the whole story. Because the F119 has a near-turbojet cycle, its military (non-afterburning) rating is a larger percentage of its maximum power than is the case for the previous generation of engines. Also, it can withstand much higher turbine temperatures, so it does not need to be throttled back as much at high speeds. At Mach 1.4, on dry thrust, the F119 generates twice as much power as the F100-PW-200.

The F-22's ventral weapon bays hold six AIM-120C AMRAAMs in the ventral bays. The side bays will each hold one AIM-9 Sidewinder missile. A General Dynamics M61A2 cannon, a lighter-weight version

The second YF-22 had Pratt & Whitney F119 engines. The Dem-Val aircraft were representative of the production design in shape, loaded weight, and power. They were heavier in terms of empty weight (limiting fuel load and endurance) and did not carry radar-absorbent material. *Lockheed Martin*

of the veteran M61 with longer, composite-wound barrels, is mounted above the right wing root. A door covers the muzzle to preserve the fighter's stealth qualities.

The F-22's stealth design evolved from the F-117, but supercomputer-driven RCS prediction techniques have allowed the designers to incorporate curves in surfaces and edges and to use RAM more sparingly. A key difference between the F-22 and earlier stealth aircraft is that the F-22 has been designed with an emphasis on balancing LO with maintenance and support costs.

The first step in reducing the amount of maintenance time spent on LO materials is to minimize the need to "break the low-observable bubble"—that is, to minimize the number of maintenance actions that involve the removal and restorations of LO coatings or seals. Where components require regular access, the F-22 has frequent-access panels with special latches and gaskets that ensure that they can be opened and closed without

breaking the bubble. In the F-117, designers tended to select the material that was best suited to the different electromagnetic, thermal, vibration, and structural requirements in any particular location—with the result that different types of material proliferated. On the F-22, the merits of each material type were balanced against a requirement to reduce the number of materials, with the result that the F-22 uses about one-third as many different LO materials as earlier stealth aircraft. This reduces inventory, logistics, training costs, and makes repair work easier.

If there is one area in which the F-22 breaks more ground than anyone expected at the start of the program, it is in avionics. The F-22 is new in so many ways that conventional sensors and displays would be inadequate. The air battle will unfold more quickly in front of the F-22 pilot, because of the fighter's greater speed. The F-22 relies on its stealth for protection against hostile air defenses, but stealth could be compromised by emissions from its own systems.

Refueling was practiced early in the YF-22 test program, making sorties longer and more productive. *Lockheed Martin*

Stealth gives the pilot a new set of variables to consider: the F-22 is more stealthy against some radars than others, and its radar reflectivity varies according to the radar's bearing. Stealth gives the F-22 the initiative in a beyond-visual-range (BVR) engagement, allowing the pilot to engage or avoid another aircraft before the F-22 can be detected.

The F-22's sensors and displays meet this challenge through a number of new techniques. "Sensor fusion" combines data from all different sensors to display one target on the screen, so that the pilot does not need to compare different displays to build up a mental picture of the battle. "Sensor management" means that the pilot does not normally have to control the radar. This is done automatically, according to the tactical situation. The sensor management function also performs emission control (EMCON) automatically, keeping electronic emissions at the lowest possible level.

In the cockpit, the center of attention is an 8x8-inch Tactical Situation Display (TSD), with 6-inch screens left, right, and below. The architecture

behind the displays is revolutionary. In today's fighters, the radar and electronic warfare (EW) systems and the communications, navigation, and identification (CNI) systems are separate, and each has its own processors. The F-22 sensors are not independent systems, but together with the displays are peripherals serving the fighter's Raytheon Common Integrated Processor (CIP), which consists of two banks of liquid-cooled computer modules housed in the forward fuselage.

The pilot's main sources of information are the TSD and the screens on either side, the left for defense, and the right for attack. These both take a subset of the data on the TSD and add more detail to it. All the screens use the same symbology and the same perspective, God's eye-view, with the F-22's track pointing up the center of the screen. The symbols are "dual-coded"—as far as possible, they differ both in shape and color. This makes them easy to distinguish and ensures that the displays will be workable even if the pilot has to wear laser-protective goggles.

Left

After experiencing problems with the sizing and construction of the F-117's rudders, Lockheed went overboard to avoid repeating the same mistakes on the YF-22, equipping it with enormous vertical tails. The later F-22A reverted to smaller surfaces. *Lockheed Martin*

Below

Under a 1986 agreement, the Air Force was to buy the A-12 and the Navy was to replace the F-14 with a version of the ATF. Lockheed's Navy ATF design used the same engines, avionics, systems, and structural technology as the F-22, but was otherwise a different airplane with a variable-sweep wing. *Lockheed Martin*

The F-22's most important sensors are the Northrop Grumman APG-77 radar and the passive electronic surveillance measures (ESM) built into the BAe Systems ALR-94 electronic warfare system.

The APG-77 and ALR-94 are unique, high-performance sensors. The APG-77 has an active, electronically scanned array (AESA) comprising some 1,200 transmitter and receiver modules. One vital difference between an AESA and any other radar that has a single transmitter is that it is capable of operating as several separate radars simultaneously. An AESA can change its beam-form very readily, and its receiver segments can operate in a passive or receive-only mode. The F-22 has space, weight, and cooling provision for auxiliary side arrays on either side of the nose. If installed, these would provide radar coverage over almost 270 degrees.

The ALR-94 is the most effective passive system ever installed on a fighter. Tom Burbage, former head of the F-22 program at Lockheed Martin, has described it as "the most technically complex piece of equipment on the aircraft." The F-22 has been described as an antenna farm—it would resemble a signals intelligence platform were it not for the fact that the 30-plus antennas are all smoothly blended into the wings and fuselage. The ALR-94 provides 360 degree coverage in all bands, with both azimuth and elevation coverage in the forward sector.

A target that is using radar to search for the F-22 or other friendly aircraft can be detected, tracked, and identified by the ALR-94 long before its radar can see anything, at ranges of 250 miles or more. As the range closes, but still above 100 miles, the APG-77 can be cued by the ALR-94 to search for

Northrop's rakish YF-23 changed very little between the award of the Dem-Val contract and first flight. Biased toward stealth and supercruise, the design was based on a pure diamond wing planform and a high degree of wing-body blending. *Northrop*

other aircraft in the hostile flight. The system uses techniques such as cued tracking. Since the track file, updated by the ALR-94, can tell the radar where to look, it can detect and track the target with a very narrow beam, measuring as little as 2 degrees by 2 degrees in azimuth and elevation. One engineer calls it "a laser beam, not a searchlight. We want to use our resources on the high-value targets—we don't track targets that are too far away to be a threat."

The system also automatically increases revisit rates according to the threat posed by the targets. Another technique is "closed-loop track-

ing," in which the radar constantly adjusts the power and number of pulses to retain a lock on its target while using the smallest possible amount of energy.

High-priority emitters—such as fighter aircraft at close range—can be tracked in real time by the ALR-94. In this mode, called narrow-band interleaved search and track (NBILST), the radar is used only to provide precise range and velocity data to set up a missile attack. If a hostile aircraft is injudicious in its use of radar, the ALR-94

Unique features of the YF-23 included underwing inlets with no diverter plates or slots, and massive V-tails for pitch and roll control. The weapon bays were built into the forward fuselage, behind the cockpit. *U.S. Air Force*

may provide nearly all the information necessary to launch an AIM-120 AMRAAM and guide it to impact, making it virtually an antiradiation AAM.

The sensor management and EMCON functions divide the airspace around the F-22 into concentric zones. In the outer zone, targets are not close enough to be a threat, and the system will not break radar silence to identify them. As they get closer and enter the "situational awareness" zone, the system is programmed to identify and track them.

The next zone is defined as that within which the F-22 pilot has the option to engage or avoid the threat. The inmost zone is bounded by the range of the threat's missiles. In each case, the system uses the radar only as much as is necessary to maintain a track. As the target gets closer, the radar will revisit it more often.

As targets are detected—whether by AWACS, the F-22's radar, or by ESM—the F-22's software assigns them to a "track file." As other sensors pick them up, the information is placed in the same track file, and the best

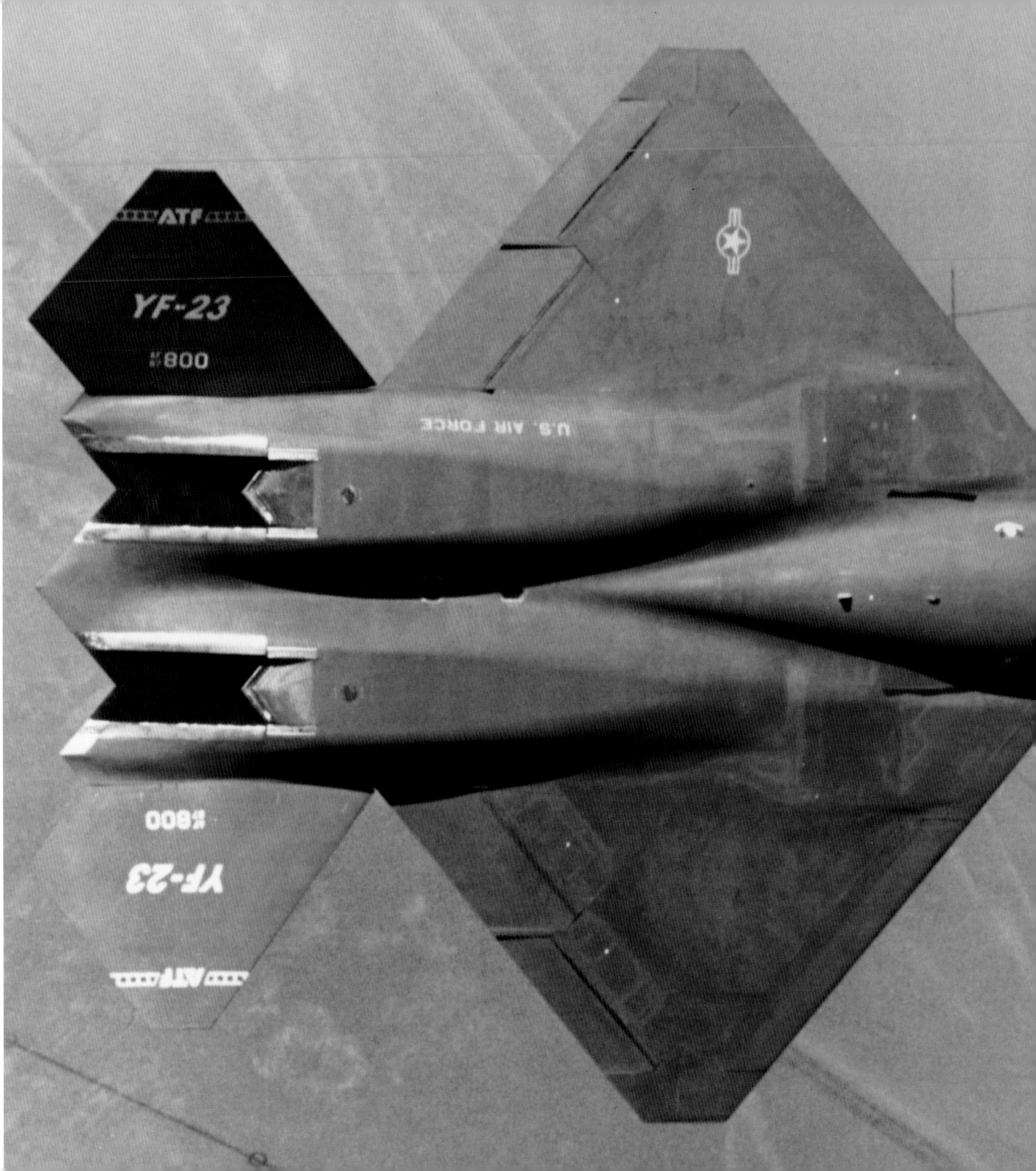
ATF
YF-23
U.S. AIR FORCE

data is drawn from the file and displayed. For instance, the display will show range and speed information acquired by the APG-77 and bearing data from the ESM.

The computers help the pilot by assembling a "shoot list," on which the targets are placed in order of priority and tracked for engagement. The attack display shows the maximum range of the F-22's own missiles—corrected for launch speed and altitude—and the lethal envelope of the target's missiles. The shoot-list function selects and arms missiles automatically.

The F-22 pilot can see when the target will be within range, and when to break off, and can use that information to decide whether to fire as soon as possible—and break away earlier—or whether to allow the range to close and give the target less chance to escape.

The F-22 was unveiled at Lockheed's Marietta plant in April 1997, and was officially named Raptor. The first flight on September 7, 1997,

The YF-23 was one of the most elegant fighter designs of any era, and many observers still believe that Northrop was robbed. One YF-23 is in storage at NASA's Dryden flight research center, and the other is displayed at the Western Museum of Flight in Los Angeles. *Northrop*

Below

The F-22 is a big airplane and has two massive engines: Pratt & Whitney F119-PW-100s, rated at some 39,000 pounds of thrust each. Great care has been taken to ensure that the engine is easy to maintain. *Pratt & Whitney*

The first engineering and manufacturing development (EMD) F-22 takes shape in Marietta. Titanium is the predominant structural material in the F-22, although high-temperature graphite-bismaleimide composites are used for many of the skins where light weight and stiffness are necessary. *Lockheed Martin*

Paul Metz taxis the F-22 out for its first flight from Marietta on September 7, 1997. Metz was also the chief test pilot for the Northrop YF-23, and declines to compare the two aircraft in public. *Bill Sweetman*

Raptor 4001 lifts off for the first time. Note the characteristic vortex trailing from the narrow-chord wingtip. This aircraft was retired in late 2000. *Bill Sweetman*

Top

The F-22's broad centerbody houses the engines, weapon bays, and most of the fighter's fuel (although the wings hold 5,000 pounds each). The inlet ducts curve to mask the engines from radar. *Bill Sweetman*

Middle

On avionics-equipped F-22s, the radome is regarded as so sensitive that people without the required security clearance are not allowed to touch it. There is space in the forward fuselage for auxiliary side-looking antennas. *Bill Sweetman*

Bottom

The F-22 is a large aircraft, similar in overall dimensions to the F-15 but more compact. The main factor driving the airplane's size is the need to carry the normal fuel and weapon load internally. *Bill Sweetman*

marked only the midpoint between the start of EMD and the fighter's entry into service.

Nine EMD aircraft are being built. Two of the 11 aircraft in the original contract were eliminated at the beginning of 1993; in 1998, however, when Congress insisted on the aircraft achieving certain test milestones before production could start, the first two production aircraft were redesigned as "production representative test vehicles" and will be used for operational testing.

The F-22 EMD aircraft will fly about as many hours as the full-scale development F-15 fleet, said program director General Mike Mushala in early 1998, but the program will be very different. "We do a lot less flying in the basic aerodynamic performance areas—with the work we do on modeling and simulation, it's really validation. We do a lot more flying on integrated avionics, LO characteristics, and supercruise." The entire program will encompass more than 2,400 flights and 4,350 hours, and will continue until 2003.

Six of the nine EMD aircraft, a modified Boeing 757 transport, and an extensive ground facility in Seattle are dedicated to avionics testing. The 757 flying test-bed (FTB) carries the F-22's Northrop Grumman APG-77 radar, a forward-mounted "wing" accommodating other F-22 antennas, a representative crew station, and 30 engineering workstations.

The first three F-22s (4001–4003) are dedicated to airframe and engine testing and weapon release clearances. The first aircraft made two flights at Marietta before being flown to Edwards aboard a C-5 in February 1998, resuming flight tests on May 17. The second aircraft flew at Marietta on June 29 and was ferried to Edwards on August 26.

Early tests showed that the F-22 was easy to fly—on its own, in formation, or in refueling—with excellent handling qualities. Pilots describe it as combining an F-16's agility with the F-15's good manners. The fighter's

Even older in concept than the AIM-9, its design dating to the 1940s, the M61 cannon is standard armament on the F-22. The installation is heavy and requires a door over the muzzle to maintain the airplane's stealth qualities. *Lockheed Martin*

power and acceleration are impressing its pilots and giving chase aircraft problems. F-15 and F-16 chases routinely use afterburner to stay with the F-22, particularly in climbs when the F-22 is close to full military power. Even at Mach 1.5, the F-22's engines are operating below military power.

In late 1998, the first two F-22s were used for a rapid envelope expansion program. The first supersonic flight was made on October 10. By the end of the year, the test team cleared the envelope to a an airspeed of Mach 1.4 (without afterburning), a peak altitude of 50,000 feet, g-loadings from +6 to -1, and an angle of attack of 26 degrees. The 1998 tests took the F-22

beyond the point—in flight hours and envelope—where major problems would usually begin to manifest themselves.

The first two aircraft have about 80 percent of full capability in terms of loads and other performance parameters, because of an overenthusiastic weight-reduction effort in the initial design. In fact, 4001 was retired to Wright-Patterson AFB in the fall of 2000, and it will be used to test the F-22's ability to survive hostile fire.

By the end of 2000, two more F-22s had flown: 4003, the first full-envelope F-22, and 4004, which carries a full set of avionics. The fighter had

An F-22 fires an AIM-9 missile during a test. The missile launch rail is carried on a trapeze, which is extended from the weapon bay. The doors must withstand exposure to the rocket blast and the Mach 1.5 airstream. *U.S. Air Force*

demonstrated excellent handling over a massive flight envelope, including altitudes above 50,000 feet and angles of attack as high as 60 degrees.

The F-22 has been controversial since EMD started in 1991. Its opponents include political budget-cutters who see it as a Cold War weapon that the United States could defer—particularly in view of the fact that there is no remotely comparable fighter on the horizon that is likely to find its way into the hands of an adversary. The United States, these opponents argue, does not need three new fighters in the early 2000s (the F-22, the F/A-18E/F Super Hornet, and the JSF). Advocates for other services quietly and not-so-quietly cite the F-22 as the answer to the wrong question. The USAF has had no difficulty establishing supremacy over other air forces, but treats the F-22 as a priority over close-support weapons that could help win the war on the ground.

In July 1999, House Republicans, led by defense appropriations chair Jerry Lewis, deleted money to build the first six production F-22s from the Fiscal Year 2000 budget. The decision would have delayed IOC for a year. It would also have added to the total cost of the program, because all the people and facilities needed to start production would have to be kept on for an extra year. But because the program is running under a Congressional limit on its total cost, the USAF would have to reduce the number of aircraft acquired. And since, when a project is cut in this way, the aircraft that are deleted are the last and least expensive production articles, the program would have lost many more than six aircraft.

Privately, senior USAF officers say that while the F-22 is important, there is a number below which the F-22 force will cost too much and be too small to sustain the USAF's air-superiority mission. The number is not publicized, and it varies according to costs and other circumstances, but it probably lies around the point where the USAF can no longer support more than two active F-22 wings of 72 operational aircraft—between 200 and 250 aircraft. In 1999, the Pentagon faced down the House committee by threatening to cancel the program if the production funds were not made available.

In a final compromise, the six aircraft were designated as test aircraft and were allowed to go ahead, as long as the test program passed a number of milestones set by the Defense Acquisition Board, by the end of 1999. The same procedure was set for 2000. A number of test events had to be accomplished, including missile firings and the testing of avionics software on Raptor 4004. As 2000 drew to a close, the team was struggling to meet that milestone after delays caused by manufacturing problems and individually minor technical snags. For instance, cracks around the canopy frame caused flight tests to be suspended for several weeks. Raptor 4004 made its first flight on November 15, 2000—six months later than planned in July

Raptor 01 rolls away from the camera. The fighter's wing area is 40 percent greater than that of the F-15, and it has 70 percent more installed power. *U.S. Air Force*

1999—raising doubts as to whether avionics tests could be performed before the end of the year.

Some USAF leaders have expressed the hope that the service will eventually buy more than the 339 F-22s planned today. With its range, speed, stealth, and advanced avionics, F-22 advocates argue, the fighter could be used as the F-117 was used at the start of the Desert Storm campaign, carrying out precision strikes against the enemy's air defense system and reducing losses among the strike force. The fighter would be particularly useful against very advanced, long-range surface-to-air missiles such as the Russian S-300V (SA-10) and S-300PMU (SA-12). Both these systems are claimed to have same capability against stealth targets; the S-300V has been exported to China and other nations, while the S-300PMU has been offered for export.

In 2000, the USAF announced that five bases had been short-listed for the first operational F-22 wing: Eglin and Tyndall in Florida; Langley in Virginia; Mountain Home in Idaho; and Elmendorf in Alaska. Langley, also the headquarters of Air Combat Command, is the Air Force's preferred site. If all goes well, the F-22 wing will declare its first squadron operational at the end of 2005—more than two decades after the first specification was issued.

Left

The first and second F-22s in formation. In early tests, these aircraft demonstrated supersonic cruise at Mach 1.5 and unprecedented climb performance. *Boeing*

Chapter 7

JSF—A STEALTH FIGHTER FOR THE WORLD?

Under just one current Pentagon project, the years after 2010 could see Lockheed Martin deliver almost 100 times more LO aircraft than the industry had built by the end of 2000. The same project could put an end to the company's career as a fighter manufacturer. Again, it could merely be an interesting footnote in the history of military aviation. As this book was written, decisions in the latter half of 2001 were expected to determine which of these vastly different outcomes would transpire.

From the viewpoint of most observers, the Joint Strike Fighter project appeared on the scene very quickly in the mid-1990s, under President Clinton's first-term administration. In 1993, the USAF and Navy had planned a number of fighter programs, including a joint-service heavy attack aircraft (A/F-X) and an F-16 replacement. By 1996, most of these had been replaced by a single new fighter that would replace thousands of Navy and USAF aircraft and, in addition, would be built in a version that could replace the Marine Corps' AV-8B Harrier short-take-off, vertical landing (STOVL) "jump-jet" fighters.

In fact, serious design work on what became the JSF had started in 1990–1991, and it had its roots in technology studies that had started several years earlier than that. In the mid-1990s, the technology met the needs of a funding-strapped military that needed a plan to replace its aircraft. It also matched the plans of an administration that did not want to start a new multi-billion dollar full-scale development program during its two terms of office.

JSF's predecessors owed their existence to two services—the U.S. Marine Corps and British Royal Navy—which flew Harriers. In the early 1980s, both had started re-equipping with new versions of the Harrier, but the services realized that they would need a replacement after 2000. Without a STOVL replacement, the Marines would go back to relying on the U.S. Navy's carrier aircraft for air support, and would no longer be able to operate jet aircraft from the Navy amphibious warfare ships. The Royal Navy's small carriers would not be able to operate conventional carrier-based aircraft at all, and would revert to helicopter carriers.

In January 1986, an international joint agreement on a Harrier replacement was signed at NASA's Ames Research Center in California. The principal parties were NASA and the U.K. Royal Aeronautical Establishment, but they worked in close collaboration with the Marines and Royal Navy, and with the U.S. and U.K. industries. The agreement covered a program

The X-35A in flight test. The JSF prototypes—or "concept demonstration aircraft" in the program's jargon—have three principal tasks: to demonstrate the basic aerodynamics of the design, to show that the carrier-based version meets basic Navy requirements, and to demonstrate the STOVL performance of the Marine version. Signature testing is being carried out on pole models, so there are no specific stealth features on the CDAs. *Lockheed Martin*

Before there was JSF, there was the U.S.–U.K. STOVL project. Lockheed had a team working on this concept, with a "tandem-fan" powerplant devised by Rolls-Royce. Some basic features of this engine—in particular, the use of a shaft to move energy to the front of the aircraft and a system that increased mass flow for powered-lift flight—were carried over to Lockheed's JSF. *Lockheed*

In 1992–1993, the air force and navy planned joint development of a two-seat attack/fighter aircraft called AFX. The Lockheed F-22 team responded with a swing-wing aircraft based on F-22 technology. *Lockheed*

that would compare several different STOVL designs against an outline requirement for a supersonic STOVL fighter. The plan was to select the most promising concepts for more detailed investigation and testing, starting in 1988, and to start development of an operational fighter in 1995.

Of the four concepts selected for development, one was a derivative of the Harrier concept with direct lift. To make the airplane hover, the engine would be installed amidships, and its thrust would be deflected downward by swiveling nozzles. Another was called a "remote augmented lift system," using a high-pressure afterburner nozzle, fixed to point downward and located in the airplane's nose. A third concept involved building large folding ejector ducts into the fighter's wing.

The Lockheed Skunk Works was part of the program, working together with Rolls-Royce on a STOVL aircraft with a "tandem-fan" engine. This was like a conventional jet engine with an extra compression stage, mounted well ahead of the rest of the engine on an extension shaft. In straight-and-level flight, the engine worked like a conventional jet. All the air would pass through the inlets, the forward compression stage, and the engine. For STOVL, though, the air through the front stage would be diverted to a pair of swiveling forward exhausts, and an extra set of inlets would open to feed the rest of the engine. In this mode, the engine acted like a high-bypass-ratio airliner engine, producing extra thrust.

By 1987, the Marines had made a key decision. The Advanced STOVL (ASTOVL) aircraft would replace both its Harriers and its conventional F/A-18s. This increased the potential size of the program to 700-plus aircraft—but it was the only good news around ASTOVL.

All the chosen designs turned out to have major problems. Problems caused by the interaction between the fighter's jet exhaust, the ground, and its inlets proved more important than expected, ruling out the afterburner-equipped direct-lift system and RALS. (When Russia's Yakovlev brought its STOVL Yak-141 to the Farnborough air show in the United Kingdom in September 1992, it hovered but did not land vertically, because it would have wrecked any surface except a steel deck.) Control of a heavy, powerful aircraft balancing on a column of air was difficult, and would extract a lot of power from the engine. Control during transition from wing-borne to jet-borne flight was particularly complex for the tandem fan and ejector. Some of the configurations were less compatible than others with stealth—but that problem could not be discussed in detail because of security concerns.

By 1989, the ASTOVL program was dead in the water. None of the concepts under study showed any promise of solving the numerous detailed problems at an acceptable level of risk.

It was during this inauspicious point in the program that the DARPA started to look at STOVL. Convinced that like stealth, a decade earlier, ASTOVL could be made feasible with a more focused, more aggressive demonstration program, DARPA set a new set of goals for the project.

DARPA's leaders eliminated most hard requirements except for a 24,000-pound maximum empty weight (a surrogate for cost). They based the project on the powerful engines developed for the YF-22 and YF-23 Advanced Tactical Fighters; laid out a program that started with the construction of a "large-scale powered model," a nonflying airplane with a complete propulsion system; and then proceeded directly into the construction and testing of a manned prototype.

The program was deliberately set up to ensure that no company would propose a solution unless it was confident that it could make it fly. Another principle—reflecting the agency's name and charter—was that preference would be given to new solutions that had not been tested before.

The Lockheed Skunk Works had such a solution in hand. Engineer Paul Bevilaqua had developed a STOVL system that was, in essence, a mechanically simpler version of the tandem-fan aircraft. The front compressor section was rotated to the horizontal position, so that it became a lifting fan. The fan's airstream was completely separate from the main engine stream, and it was no longer used in up-and-away flight. Instead, it was disconnected from the engine by a clutch and its inlet and exhaust were covered by doors.

The new STOVL system had some inherently useful features. Its drive shaft, powered by a turbine at the rear of the engine, literally extracted energy from the rear of the airplane and converted it into vertical thrust at the front, balancing the airplane in hovering flight. Also, the front-to-rear thrust balance could be adjusted quickly—without waiting for engine components to spin up—by adjusting guide vanes in the fan and the area of the turbine nozzle. The lift fan exhaust velocity was comfortably low, and it reduced energy and velocity in the main engine exhaust. This was potentially important with the high-thrust ATF engines. The exhaust striking the ground could expand in the form of a high-velocity sheet, turning inert objects into lethal missiles. (One discovery in early British STOVL experiments was that the exhaust

The F-22-based AFX would have had larger internal weapon bays than the F-22, and smaller engines—the PW7000, based on the F119. By the time the design was unveiled in 1994, hopes that it would enter production were slim. *Lockheed*

sheet generated a low-pressure zone directly above the ground, and—consequently—a pressure differential between the tops and bottoms of manhole covers that was sufficient to get them airborne.)

The Lockheed project was an early favorite of the DARPA managers. Another was a fan-lift design from McDonnell Douglas, which was similar except that the fan was driven by a turbine, spun by hot gas tapped from the main engine.

As DARPA refined its requirement, with the goal of starting its demonstration programs in 1993, and Lockheed worked on the new STOVL concept, another lightbulb went on. Unlike the Harrier, the fan-lift STOVL designs had a basically conventional internal layout with the engine in the back. If the fan and its hardware were removed, the area behind the cockpit would accommodate a large fuel tank, and the result would be a fighter with an unusually large internal fuel fraction and hence an excellent range. For the USAF, one of the lessons of Desert Storm was that it needed more range in its fighters if it was not going to fight in Central Europe. The DARPA planners started to see the ASTOVL aircraft as a potential replacement for the F-16.

By the time DARPA issued contracts to Lockheed and McDonnell Douglas in March 1993, the project was not only ASTOVL but the

NASA LANGLEY
16 FOOT TRANSONIC TUNNEL

Another program that was buried in the 1993–1994 defense cuts was the Multi-Role Fighter (MRF). This is a McDonnell Douglas concept for what was to have been the F-16 replacement, under test in a NASA wind tunnel in 1993. *NASA*

Common Affordable Lightweight Fighter (CALF). By this time, DARPA had identified funding for a complete program. Both companies would build powered models at near-full-scale. In 1995, DARPA would pick one candidate for a flight demonstration program, in conventional take-off and landing (CTOL) version and ASTOVL form.

Meanwhile, in September 1993, the incoming Clinton administration axed the individual services' future fighter programs—the USAF/Navy A/F-X long-range attack aircraft and the USAF's Multi-Role Fighter (MRF), intended as the replacement for the F-16. As a meager consolation prize, the Pentagon established a new program called Joint Advanced Strike Technology (JAST),

Right

Under the DARPA-sponsored Common Affordable Lightweight Fighter (CALF) program, Lockheed built this large-scale powered model of the company's design. Aimed at the requirements of the Marines and Air Force, it had a canard configuration and greater wing sweep than the later JSF. *Lockheed*

The Yakovlev Yak-141 was the only supersonic STOVL design under development when CALF started. Taking advantage of the end of the Cold War, Lockheed licensed the design of its three-bearing exhaust nozzle and used it on JSF.

Right
McDonnell Douglas' CALF design was a stealthy canard with definite echoes of the YF-23—on which McDonnell Douglas had been Northrop's teammate. It was designed around a GE F120 engine, and a GE-developed lift fan driven by hot gas from the engine compressor. *McDonnell Douglas*

intended to look at weapons, avionics, and other technologies for new-generation strike aircraft. Within a few months, a tidy-minded Congress had discovered CALF and transferred it from DARPA to the newly formed JAST office.

What happened in the next few months was dramatic and unexpected. Under the leadership of Major General George Muellner, a fighter pilot who had once commanded the 6513th Test Wing at Area 51, the JAST office assembled a massive program around the CALF designs. Muellner's vision was of a "universal fighter" that could cover all the services' different needs in a largely common airframe. It would be made possible by precision weapons— like the F-117, it would put two bombs in the right place and would not need a multibomb internal load like the A-12—and advanced avionics. New manufacturing and design techniques would make it affordable.

Boeing surprised its competitors with a determined run at the JSF requirement. The company issued this vague and misleading drawing in 1992; in fact, Boeing was working on a small, compact aircraft with a lower empty weight than the F-16, and upturned wingtips. *Boeing*

Using the latest computer mission-modeling and campaign-level simulation techniques, the JAST office coordinated a tough session of trading among the three services. The Navy was persuaded to accept a single-engine, single-seat aircraft. The Air Force agreed to accept an airplane that would be slower and less agile than the F-22—in fact, not much faster or more maneuverable than the F-16. The result was an airplane that accomplished the critical elements of the services' missions but was still small enough to form the basis of a practical STOVL aircraft.

In an interview in April 1995, Muellner said that the customers had converged on a family of closely similar designs, differing mainly in the way that they landed and took off. The industrial implications were enormous. The Marines wanted to replace 600 older aircraft, the Navy needed 300 aircraft, and the USAF could replace almost 2,000 F-16s. Never had such a massive program been created so fast. Moreover, JAST looked like the only U.S. tactical aircraft program that would start before 2010—and was also being billed as the worldwide replacement for 2,000-plus F-16s and F/A-18s.

In 1986, seven companies had submitted proposals for the ATF Dem/Val phase. By late 1994, four companies were ready to compete in JAST—Grumman had been acquired by Northrop, General Dynamics had been absorbed by Lockheed (which was itself in the process of merging

In tests of the Lockheed Martin large-scale powered model at NASA's Ames Research Center, paint was used to show how the air would flow along the ground. The line of yellow dots under the midfuselage shows how the lift-fan efflux forms a barrier that keeps hot core exhaust away from the inlets. *Lockheed*

with Martin-Marietta), and Rockwell had virtually left the military aircraft business. The two companies to be eliminated in 1996 would be out of the picture as combat aircraft primes.

Lockheed and McDonnell Douglas already had their DARPA-era contracts. Both companies had chosen stealthy canard (tail-first) designs. Boeing, meanwhile, had funded its own fighter studies in parallel, producing an extraordinary design that was almost a flying wing, with its propulsion system and weapons in an underwing nacelle, and wingtip-mounted fins. Northrop Grumman produced a canard design with a separate lift engine rather than an engine-driven fan, and, in 1994, joined British Aerospace on the McDonnell Douglas team.

Lockheed Martin unveiled a revised JAST design in late 1995. The major difference stemmed from the Navy's carrier-landing requirements. A carrier-based aircraft must be able to fly slowly in a flat attitude—which implies a generous wing span and effective flaps—and must feature responsive and precise control at low speeds. As Lockheed Martin adapted the canard design to these requirements, the canard became awkwardly big.

Anticanard prejudice played a role. Lockheed had relocated the JAST program to Fort Worth, where F-16 designer Harry Hillaker had long taught that

Lockheed's powered model was tested in the 40x80-foot wind tunnel at NASA Ames. Although the JSF design was changed to a tail-aft configuration, data from tests of the STOVL system was still valid. *Lockheed Martin*

"the optimum location for a canard is on somebody else's airplane." In 1995, the canard Eurofighter Typhoon was sitting on the ground while its designers wrestled with flight-control problems, and the Saab Gripen's developers were dealing with a rash of handling gremlins. All in all, the Lockheed Martin team felt that there was enough risk in the JAST program without adding a canard to the mix.

This small unmanned research vehicle, the McDonnell Douglas X-36, was a subscale model of a highly stealthy, agile supersonic fighter design related to the company's CALF project. It had no vertical surfaces at all, directional control being provided by a secret vectored-thrust nozzle with no external moving parts. *McDonnell Douglas*

McDonnell Douglas, Northrop Grumman, and British Aerospace teamed up in 1995 to propose a JSF design with a separate lift engine and a wing planform similar to that of the X-36. *McDonnell Douglas*

By 1996, the McDonnell Douglas design had evolved into a near-tailless configuration with an all-axis vectoring nozzle and shallow V-tails. *McDonnell Douglas*

Lockheed Martin's first Joint Strike Fighter demonstrator, the X-35A/B, under construction at Palmdale. Both X-35s were identical at this stage of assembly. Both have a bay behind the cockpit to accommodate the lift fan, and the basic wing structure is the same; the Navy X-35C has larger flaps and wingtips. *Lockheed Martin*

Lockheed Martin looked at a pure delta wing. At one point, the company was looking at a delta for the USMC, USAF, and RN and a tailed configuration for the U.S. Navy—but the final design echoed the F-22, with four tails and a cropped delta wing. One huge advantage of this design was that it drew on the extensive and flight-validated database from the F-22 program. Data from the large-scale powered model, unveiled in April 1995 and tested at NASA Ames, was still applicable.

In March 1996, the JAST office released an RFP for the JAST prototypes, with a deadline in early June. Shortly afterward, the project's name changed from JAST to the Joint Strike Fighter (JSF), reflecting the fact that it was backed by an operational requirement. Three companies responded. Boeing and Lockheed Martin had talked about teaming, but neither wanted to give up its own design, so they competed with McDonnell Douglas' team.

JSF avionics prototypes have been test-flown aboard this BAC One-Eleven transport, owned by Northrop Grumman. Revolutionary, low-cost sensors are a key part of the effort to reduce costs in the new fighter. *Lockheed Martin*

Most people expected that Lockheed Martin and the McDonnell Douglas team would win. McDonnell Douglas had massive experience with STOVL and Navy fighters on its side, together with Northrop Grumman's stealth expertise. Add up the total of manned supersonic aircraft, jet fighters, and stealth aircraft built by Boeing—and the number was zero.

But it had taken McDonnell Douglas several months to organize its "dream team," spread across the United Kingdom, St. Louis, and California. It made a late change from the jet-driven fan to a separate lift engine—a solution that many people in the JAST office did not like. Lockheed Martin's design, with its close relationship to the F-22, looked like a low-risk solution; the McDonnell Douglas design was quite similar, but the Boeing proposal was different and definitely riskier. In previous two-track flight demonstration programs, the winners conformed to a pattern. They would be different, and one would be low-risk and the other adventurous. This logic prevailed, and Lockheed Martin and Boeing were selected for the next phase of JSF in November 1996.

McDonnell Douglas' erstwhile teammates, BAe and Northrop Grumman, joined the Lockheed Martin team. McDonnell Douglas, facing the near-extinction of its commercial airplane business and stunned by its defeat in JSF, negotiated a takeover by Boeing.

The roadmap for the JSF competition resembled nothing as much as a map of Grand Central Station, with dozens of parallel tracks converging on a single outcome, selection of a winning team, initially planned for the spring of 2001.

Taking the highest profile was the Concept Demonstration Aircraft (CDA) program. Lockheed Martin and Boeing would each build two test aircraft. Their most important task would be to demonstrate STOVL. Only one of each pair would be delivered as a STOVL aircraft, but the other would be able to be converted into STOVL form in the event of a mishap. They would also be used for some conventional envelope-expansion testing, and to show that the teams could produce an acceptable carrier-capable (CV) version, but these were seen as much less risky areas.

The CDA prototypes were given X-vehicle designations (Boeing X-32 and Lockheed Martin X-35) to underline the fact that they were experimental prototypes focused on a single technology. In 1996, the JSF requirement was by no means final, but the design of the CDA aircraft nevertheless had to begin, and there would be no time to change the CDAs as the requirement evolved. Consequently, the program office wanted to ensure that the final designs would not be chained to the CDA configuration, and calling them X-vehicles rather than "YF-" prototypes was part of that process.

Wind-tunnel model of the Lockheed Martin JSF's new "diverterless" inlet. The combination of the raked-forward outer lip and the bulged inner wall deflects the turbulent boundary layer above and below the inlet, eliminating splitter plates and suction devices. *Lockheed Martin*

Left
Another full-scale JSF model has been used at Fort Worth to evaluate sensors and antennas and their location on the airframe. *Lockheed Martin*

The CDAs are not intended to be stealthy, but their basic external shapes conform to stealth principles. As in the case of Have Blue and the ATF, the teams had to model their stealth technology on computers and then build full-scale models for tests on ground-based RCS ranges. Since the days of ATF, both teams have improved their RCS facilities to detect smaller echoes and gather a more accurate picture of the model; also, the models built under JSF are more detailed than ever before.

In addition to flying the CDAs, the competing teams would design the new fighter's avionics suite and test its essential elements on the ground and in flight, aboard flying test-bed aircraft. The JSF office also picked out some specific new technologies that promised to make the aircraft less costly to build and maintain. For example, a USAF/industry team had been working for some years on what was called a "more electric airplane," in which electric motors and actuators would replace some or all of the hydraulics. The JSF program took over this work, injected more money, and accelerated it. The work was divided between the competing teams, but all data would be available to both designs.

Lockheed Martin's JSF SigMA Signature Measurement Aircraft is the highest-fidelity RCS model that the company has ever built, allowing accurate RCS measurement of small details of the shape, complete with absorbent coatings. It is seen here on Lockheed Martin's company RCS range at Helendale, California. *Lockheed Martin*

Other common elements included the engine design. Given the pressure of time and the fact that the F119 was well into development for the F-22, Pratt & Whitney was chosen to build F119-based engines for the CDA. The company was also selected to develop a production engine, but General Electric, Allison, and Rolls-Royce were awarded contracts to start work on an alternate engine.

The design of the production JSF and all its components and support systems—known as the "preferred weapon system concept" or PWSC—proceeded in parallel with the CDA design, and went hand-in-hand with the definition of the final requirement.

In 1996, the different services had set different values—usually, a "minimum" and a "desired" value in each case—for range, weapon load, stealth, and every other feature of the airplane. Under Muellner's leadership, the JSF office had designed a process that would, over a four-year period, engineer a compromise; while the services had not signed a definitive set of requirements in 1996, they had agreed on that process.

The JSF requirement would be hammered out in four one-year cycles. The customers would agree on a draft of a "joint interim requirements document" or JIRD. The contractors would respond with changes to their PWSC designs. If a change in the JIRD cost too much to meet, the requirement might be revised until a final JIRD was devised at the end of the cycle. Then, another JIRD would be issued. Each JIRD focused on different areas (observables, avionics, and weapons, for example). The final product would be a Joint Operational Requirements Document, or JORD, issued in early 2000. This would be the specification for JSF and the basis for the final showdown.

The overriding principle was "cost as an independent variable," or CAIV. The underlying assumption behind the JSF program was that the three major customers would not reduce the size of their fighter forces. This would be unaffordable unless the cost of the new fighter was rigidly controlled. Consequently, the only rigidly fixed element of the JSF specification was cost. With each JIRD cycle, if some capability (stealth, for instance) started to force the cost above the goal, something else had to be traded off, or done more cheaply, to compensate for it.

A vital tool in the process was simulation. As the JIRD requirements and the PWSC designs evolved, the changes were tested in engineering simulators to show how the performance of the aircraft changed. Those results were plugged into campaign-level simulations—real-time wargames, often using netted computers thousands of miles apart—to show how the changes to the design would translate into targets killed or airplanes lost in wartime.

Within Lockheed Martin, the management of the JSF program was assigned to Fort Worth. In the early 1990s, the F-16 program leaders had successfully dealt with the abrupt post–Cold War crash in production rates, when annual F-16 output plummeted from a peak of 180 aircraft a year to barely double-digit numbers. Not only did the division survive, but it even reduced its costs. Fort Worth—with management of the JSF and the continuing F-16 program, and a large share of F-22—became the center of Lockheed Martin's "fighter enterprise." However, the CDAs would be built at the Skunk Works in Palmdale.

The X-35 is clearly a cousin to the F-22. The basic aerodynamics are similar, and the two aircraft take the same approach to stealth, with a combination of flat and curved surfaces and a sharp chine around the perimeter of the airframe. The main differences between the two aircraft (apart from size and the single engine) are the X-35's new "diverterless" inlet, with a bump on the inner wall rather than a splitter plate, and the axisymmetrical nozzle. Unlike the F-22, the X-35 does not use thrust vectoring in up-and-away flight.

The JSF lacks the larger F-22's "cheek" missile bays. Instead, it has two bays to the left and right of the keel, each with two doors. The inner door in

Cost-saving measures in Lockheed Martin's JSF design include the use of adhesive film to replace paint. The film is easier to remove and replace than paint, with fewer environmental problems. *Lockheed Martin*

each bay carries a launch rail for an AIM-120 AMRAAM. The outer door is slightly bulged on the Navy and USAF versions to accommodate a 900-kilogram weapon. The wing includes four hardpoints, rated at 5,000 pounds inboard and 2,500 pounds outboard.

The STOVL version is externally identifiable by a slight bulge in the spine, and a shorter canopy. The lift fan, developed by Allison Advanced Development Company (AADC), is located behind the cockpit in a bay with upper and lower clamshell doors. The lift fan has two counterrotating stages and supports almost half the airplane's weight in hovering flight, producing 18,000 pounds thrust. The lift fan doubles the mass flow of the propulsion system, and boosts its thrust by 44 percent. The lift-fan drive shaft is engaged by a computer-controlled clutch with carbon pads, and delivers a total of 27,000 shaft horsepower to the fan—equivalent to the propeller shaft of an Aegis-class cruiser.

Air from the engine fan feeds two roll control ducts that extend out to the wing fold line. The core exhaust flows through a "three-bearing" nozzle, developed by Rolls-Royce using data acquired from Russia's Yakovlev design bureau, which flew such a nozzle in 1990 on its Yak-141 prototype. The exhaust duct has a near-circular section and includes two control—but they do not operate like Harrier controls. The STOVL control does not select nozzle angle, but it is a mode control. In its forward (down) position, the airplane is configured for horizontal flight. Pulling the lever back to mid-position prepares the aircraft for transition, opening doors and starting the lift fan, and causes a continuously computed hover point to appear on the pilot's helmet-mounted display. The pilot pulls the lever back to the vertical position, and the aircraft automatically slows into a hover. At this point, the throttle no longer directly commands engine thrust, but becomes a vertical velocity controller. The pilot positions the aircraft over the desired landing point and pulls back on the throttle to shut down.

Making it this simple for the pilot is nightmarishly complicated for the software, which must coordinate a switch from aerodynamic to propulsion-controlled flight that is so smooth that the pilot is unaware that it is happening. In the hover, the system juggles the throttle, roll nozzles, the angle of the final nozzle, the cascades on the fan, and the fan guide vanes to keep the aircraft stable. Software integrity is crucial. Even the smallest software burp could cause an engine transient large enough to lose the aircraft.

A key challenge in the design of the JSF is to meet different service requirements without building three different aircraft. The most extreme

The serpentine inlet ducts of a stealth aircraft can be very expensive to produce. On Lockheed Martin's JSF design, they are bonded composite structures with no fasteners, sharply reducing costs. *Lockheed Martin*

wedge-shaped segments that rotate in opposite directions, bending the duct through 100 degrees. Differential rotation can also be used to deflect the exhaust from side to side. Another distinguishing feature of the STOVL version is an auxiliary inlet for the main engine, above the fuselage.

One of the advantages of this system, compared to a direct-lift system, such as the Harrier or Boeing X-32, is that pitch and roll control can be accomplished by modulating the thrust of the four lift "posts," rather than by bleeding air (and power) from the engine to a dedicated control system. Valves in the roll ducts open and close differentially for roll control. In the pitch axis, energy can be switched between the engine exhaust nozzle and the fan by adjusting the main engine's exhaust nozzle and the inlet guide vanes on the fan. Total thrust and efficiency remain unchanged.

A difference between the Lockheed Martin JSF and the Harrier is that the powered-lift system is controlled automatically. Like the Harrier, the JSF pilot has three hand controls—stick, throttle, and a dedicated STOVL

The Air Force and Navy versions of the Lockheed Martin JSF will be fitted with a low-observable axisymmetrical nozzle (LOAN) developed by Pratt & Whitney. It is designed to meet JSF stealth requirements while costing and weighing less than the nozzles of the F-22. It is seen here under test on an F-16. *Lockheed Martin*

Above

The Air Force's long-serving Advanced Fighter Technology Integration (AFTI) F-16 has flown in support of the JSF's power-by-wire or "more electric" technology. The JSF will use electrical power to move flight controls and perform other functions, eliminating maintenance-heavy, vulnerable hydraulic lines. *Lockheed Martin*

Below

Boeing's first X-32 prototype nears completion at Palmdale in late 1999. The unique Boeing design is based on a deep-section, one-piece delta wing, which contains the fuel and main landing gear and bears most of the flight loads. The nacelle under the fuselage contains the engine and weapon bays, and the forebody comprises the cockpit, inlet, and nose. *Boeing*

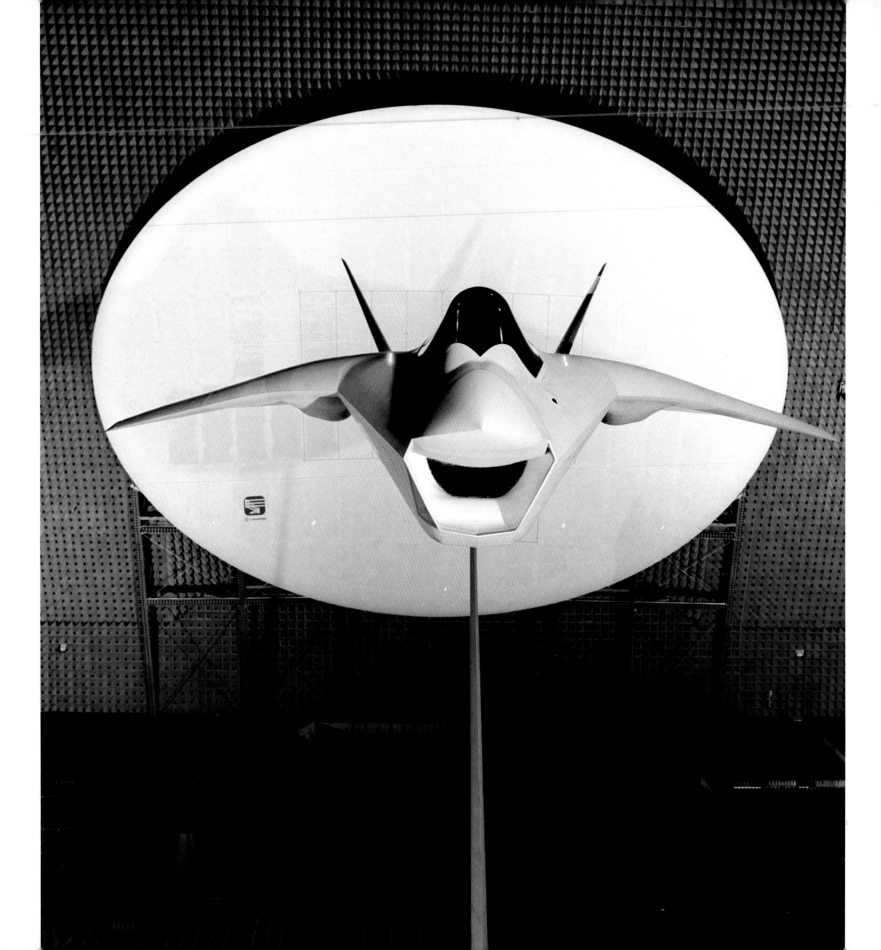

DANGER➡
ENGINE INLET

Unlike any other fighter since the 1940s, the Boeing JSF has its engine installed ahead of the center of gravity. Here, an F119 engine is being installed in the first X-32. The lower door of the right-hand weapon bay is open. *Boeing*

Left
Boeing, like Lockheed, built a high-fidelity RCS model, but has done most of its testing indoors, in a sophisticated, highly secure indoor RCS range built in 1986. The oval shape behind the aircraft is a large and precisely shaped reflector that collimates (that is, focuses to infinity) the beams of radar emitters set into the floor of the range. Notably airbrushed-out are the intimate details of the inlet duct, where Boeing has done something unusual to conceal the engine from radar. *Boeing*

requirements are imposed by the Marines and the U.S. Navy. The principal issue in the Marine design (apart from the STOVL system itself) is weight. If the operating empty weight grows too much during development, the airplane may not be able to land vertically with reserve fuel and weapons. The Navy is more concerned with aerodynamic lift and control. A carrier-based aircraft needs to be able to control its descent rate responsively on approach. This tends to require a large wing, fitted with effective flaps, and a large stabilizer.

Lockheed Martin has addressed the different requirements by changing the wing and tail sizes. The carrier variant's wing and tail are some 40 percent larger than those of the USAF and Marine versions. The CV airplane's wing has separate flaps and ailerons—the USAF and Marine aircraft have one-piece flaperons like the F-16. The smaller wing

The X-35A in high-speed taxi tests. The doors that close off the lift-fan bay are visible behind the cockpit. *Lockheed Martin*

Below

The Lockheed Martin X-35A runs up its engine in preparation for its first flight. All four JSF prototypes—Boeing's X-32s and the X-35s—have Pratt & Whitney F119 engines, specially modified to suit their STOVL systems. A General Electric/Rolls-Royce engine will be available as an alternative for production aircraft. *Lockheed Martin*

of the STOVL and USAF aircraft will save weight and (to some extent) improve speed and acceleration.

Computer-aided design and manufacture plays an important part in optimizing the different designs for their missions. Computer-based design techniques make it faster and less expensive to redesign components and structures to carry different loads. For example, the Lockheed Martin JSF's body includes several large transverse bulkheads that carry the wings and main landing gear. The CV version's longer wings impose larger bending loads on the bulkhead, and the landing gear mounts have to absorb the impact of a carrier landing—even a bad one. With computer-aided design, it is possible to design different bulkheads for the different versions, with more metal where it is needed. With computer-driven manufacturing systems, a single flexible machining station can build a CV bulkhead in one operation, and a STOVL component in the next, without any outside adjustment. The aim is to reduce what the designers call "scar weight"—extra material that is required only for one version but is carried by all three.

Cutting the cost of building the JSF airframe is important; but propulsion and avionics account for at least as large a portion of the initial investment. When it comes to maintenance and support, they are even more important.

Engine development is relatively straightforward. The JSF will not supercruise as fast as the F-22 (if at all), reducing the sustained temperatures in the heart of the engine. To produce the JSF engine, both Pratt & Whitney and the GE team will be able to replace some parts of the original F119 and F120 with lower-temperature materials. Moreover, the quest for lower operating costs and better performance in commercial engines has reached the point where military and commercial engines use the same parts and share the same low-cost supply chains.

The avionics challenge has been tougher—and can basically be summed up as bringing military aircraft into the PC era and achieving a huge step forward in the relationship of cost and performance. The final JSF requirement defines a set of sensors, processors, and displays that, in themselves, will greatly improve the fighter's effectiveness and versatility.

In 1983, McDonnell Douglas cockpit design leader Gene Adam—who was responsible for the original F/A-18 cockpit, which set a pattern for a generation—presented a visionary cockpit concept that he called Big Picture. The entire instrument panel became an electronic display screen. The main display could be a highly detailed map, showing threats, targets, and waypoints, or it could be a perspective view that showed terrain and defenses. Smaller windows could show the output of sensors such as IR cameras. The head-up display was gone, replaced by a helmet-mounted system that allowed the pilot to see and to cue weapons in all directions. In 1983, not even Gene Adam knew how such a system could be made to work. The only way it could even be simulated involved a big-screen TV and a file-cabinet-size electronic image generator.

In 2000, Big Picture lives and is a basic part of JSF, with some enhancements that even Gene Adam did not quite dare to predict.

The Lockheed Martin JSF main display measures 8 inches deep by 20 inches across. It is produced by Rockwell Collins (formerly Kaiser) and uses the same technology that is used in LCD projectors for business presentations. The basic display is a digital map, overlaid with ground and air threats and targets, and hosts a Windows-like interface that allows the pilot to access system information and imagery. The pilot has a wide-angle, binocular helmet-mounted display (HMD) also from Rockwell Collins, which can superimpose both symbols and images over the outside world.

The displays are fed with information from a battery of sources. Threats and target data can be stored on an onboard database—the mission plan is loaded with a card, of the same kind used on a laptop computer—received from other aircraft via a datalink, or detected by the fighter's onboard sensors.

The sensor suite represents a considerable step forward in capability. The electronic warfare system, provided by BAe Systems and Litton, not only detects threats but identifies them and locates them in both bearing and range—a capability that was previously confined to heavy and expensive specialized systems carried on electronic jamming aircraft. The system is accurate enough to allow the JSF to attack the emitter with a GPS-guided weapon. The forward-looking active radar array also acts as a sensitive passive listening device and can be employed as a very powerful jammer; the arrays being designed for JSF weigh one-quarter as much as they would have using 1995 technology.

Perhaps the single most spectacular new sensor on JSF is the "staring" infrared system. Arranged around the JSF are six solid-state, focal-plane-array IR sensors, each with a 60-degree x 60-degree field of view, providing spherical coverage around the aircraft. The sensors have three basic functions. They warn of approaching missiles, detect and track aircraft at long range, and feed the HMD with imagery. The pilot can see IR imagery in any direction, even through the floor of the airplane—something that will be particularly valuable in vertical landings.

The system will make the greatest possible use of commercial, off-the-shelf (COTS) technology. This is a big change from the F-22. When the Raptor was designed, its avionics system demanded computer technology that pushed the state of the art in size and performance. As a result, it was built with components that were expensive and unique. Now, they are outperformed by the high-speed chips in the newest desktop computers, and are almost impossible to manufacture. JSF designers are trying to avoid this kind of obsolescence by building their systems to commercial standards; as faster and better commercial components are developed, the JSF system should be able to use them.

Lockheed Martin's competitor takes a similar approach to many subsystems and technologies—but has a very different configuration. Boeing's JSF design underwent a major change in late 1998, switching from a delta wing to a four-tail configuration. But some basic and revolutionary

The X-35A banks above the Mojave desert with the gear extended. Contrary to first impressions, the augmentor is not lit: the F119 runs hotter than most engines and a visible glow is apparent even in military power. *Lockheed Martin*

Left

Tom Morgenfeld lifts off in the X-35A for the fighter's first flight on October 24, 2000. The X-35A was used to demonstrate the basic handling of the Air Force variant of the JSF. *Lockheed Martin*

characteristics of the company's design have remained constant. The wing is the primary element of the structure, comprises a single tip-to-tip assembly, and has an unusually thick section. The fuselage nacelle is attached underneath it.

Boeing has changed from a delta to a less-tapered trapezoidal wing, but has retained the same 55-degree leading-edge sweep. This is important for two reasons. First, the high sweep angle makes it possible to use a very thick section without excessive transonic drag—with the result that the one-piece wing, spanning only 30 feet (9.15 meters) on the STOVL aircraft, accommodates 20,000 pounds of fuel. Second, the sweep angle is favorable for installing communications and electronic warfare antennas that have a good field of regard, but which do not cause RCS problems.

The STOVL version's wing extends less than 10 feet (3 meters) on each side of the body. The USAF's CTOL version and the Navy's CV aircraft have 3 feet (90 centimeters) more wing on each side, with cambered

Although the X-35 resembles the F-22 in many respects, there are some key differences. In particular, the wing is smaller in proportion to the aircraft and less sharply swept, and the body is relatively stout. JSF is more of a bomber than a fighter. *Lockheed Martin*

Right

Marine Corps Major Art Tomassetti gets the traditional first-flight treatment after his first sortie in the X-35A. For the occasion, the fan inlet and exhaust doors above and below the fuselage are open, as are the doors that cover the auxiliary inlet for the main engine *Lockheed Martin*

Left

After only a month of flight testing, the X-35A exceeded Mach 1. It was then returned to Palmdale, where it was to be fitted with the lift-fan and other components of the powered-lift system before returning to flight tests as the X-35B. *Lockheed Martin*

The X-35C, representative of the U.S. Navy JSF, takes off on its first flight on December 16, 2000. It has a larger wing than the X-35A/B (on which the wingspan is limited by the need to fit Royal Navy carriers) and separate ailerons. *Lockheed Martin*

Left
Refueling was practiced early in the flight-test program, and was used to ferry the X-35C to Patuxent River for carrier-suitability tests. *Lockheed Martin*

leading edges and leading-edge flaps on the outer wing sections. The wing has a titanium structure and composite skins. There is no wing folding. Boeing says that it is a typical example of the complexity that the operator does not want.

Under the wing is a nacelle that contains the engine and the weapon bays, with a two-dimensional thrust-vectoring nozzle at the back and a yawning inlet—it can swallow 400 pounds of air every second—at the front. Inside the inlet is another surprise: there is the front of the engine, located just to the rear of the cockpit. The Boeing JSF is the first fighter with its engine in the front since a few early jets of the 1940s were modified from piston-engine fighters.

The engine is in the front because that puts the exhaust in the middle, close to the center of gravity. The Boeing JSF has no lift fan. The aft nozzle closes down, and butterfly valves behind the engine open to let the exhaust through two small, swiveling, retractable nozzles between and below the weapon bays. A special "jet screen" nozzle—a transverse slit just ahead of the main nozzles—generates a fan of air that is tailored to keep hot air from

continued on page 146

The JSF competitors stood nose-to-nose in November 2000 at Edwards Air Force Base. The contrast in design approaches is remarkable. *Bill Sweetman*

The front view of the X-32 is dominated by the enormous inlet. The central mystery of the design is how Boeing has contrived to reduce the head-on RCS without any apparent means of blocking the line-of-sight to the engine's compressor face. *Bill Sweetman*

The Boeing powerplant installation is unique. The engine itself is located forward, and is connected by a spool duct section to the augmentor and nozzle, located in the tail. The nozzle design on the X-32 prototypes is based on F-22 hardware. *Bill Sweetman*

Although Boeing's JSF Preferred Weapon System Concept PWSC design has a separate tail, its wing design will not be unlike that of the X-32A. With 55 degrees of sweep, the leading edge can be physically thick while offering low drag. The deep, fixed section inboard of the leading-edge flap will hold many of the fighter's electronic warfare and communications antennas. *Bill Sweetman*

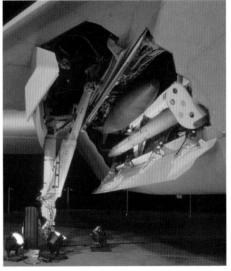

The X-32A has one operating weapon bay. It is designed to accommodate one air-to-surface store (in the widest part of the nacelle just below the wing) and an AIM-120 AMRAAM below it. Both weapons are carried on a pair of swing arms, which move outward and downward. *Bill Sweetman*

Left

The Boeing JSF design features a two-dimensional nozzle in the tail. On the PWSC design, the nozzle will be integrated into the airframe and is expected to be lighter than the engine-mounted nozzles of the F-22. *Bill Sweetman*

Continued from page 143

The Boeing JSF may not look like a classic supersonic fighter design. Its performance equation, however, combines enormous engine thrust (the fighter's modified and refanned engine provides more than 34,000 pounds of thrust without reheat—equivalent to the maximum augmented thrust of an F/A-18) with relatively low empty weight, very large internal fuel capacity, and internal stores carriage, which reduces cruise drag. The basic airframe may not be a model of aerodynamic efficiency—but in clean condition it will have much lower drag than a conventional fighter carrying an equivalent fuel and weapon load.

A Boeing weapons-bay mockup shows the swing arms in the extended position. The AMRAAM can be ejected directly through the lower door, and the swing arms move out to release the bomb. *Bill Sweetman*

Right
Boeing's X-32A performs a simulated carrier approach at Edwards Air Force Base, using every available lifting device. Trailing-edge and leading-edge flaps are full down, and the unique "apex flaps" above the inner leading edge, which trap the leading-edge vortex and trim the airplane nose up, are in the up position. *Boeing*

The X-32A on an early test flight. This view emphasizes the design's key feature—its large one-piece wing—which will be carried over into the PWSC configuration. *Boeing*

On the Boeing JSF, the weapon bays are located on each side of the spool duct that connects the engine with the combined augmentor and up-and-away nozzle. One advantage of the side-mounted bays is that the JSF can release weapons from the bay that faces away from the closest threat radar, avoiding a telltale RCS spike.

The most interesting detail that Boeing won't talk about is how the designers have masked the radar return from the engine face. The inlet duct itself does not provide line-of-sight blockage (as the longer ducts on the Lockheed F-22 and JSF do). An axial-flow baffle, of the type used on the F/A-18E/F Super Hornet, may be used, but such devices are acknowledged to cause a performance loss—which no STOVL aircraft can afford—and are generally not considered to match the LO characteristics of a serpentine duct. ("A key feature of a stealth aircraft is a serpentine inlet," charged a Lockheed executive at the Farnborough air show in July 2000. "Look at aircraft

that claim to be LO and see if they have that or not.")

One possibility is that Boeing has devised a variable-geometry baffle that can provide optimum LO characteristics for ingress and attack, and high performance for air combat (when the aircraft has by definition been detected) and vertical landing. Another option is a new and more efficient design of fixed baffle. There is clearly something in there, since Boeing's head-on views of the JSF radar cross-section model have been censored to obscure the inlet duct; if it works from both the aerodynamic and RCS standpoints, it is a very important accomplishment.

At the end of 2000, the JSF program faces a critical year, with two completely different challenges. On the technical side, the crunch item is STOVL testing.

Boeing was first into the air; its CTOL and carrier-configured (CV)

The X-32 with weapon-bay doors open, with an AMRAAM and a Joint Direct Attack Munition visible. Despite the fighter's proportions, Boeing says that its drag is low because of wing sweep and the lack of external stores. *Boeing*

Right

"Functional" and "unconventional" are two words that could describe the X-32, although the design is carefully thought-out and practical. For example, the arrangement of the weapon bays allows the pilot to launch a weapon from the side that faces away from the nearest radar, reducing the likelihood of detection. *Boeing*

As this book closes for press, the X-32 and X-35 are being prepared for crucial tests of their STOVL characteristics—and the new Bush administration is reviewing the question of whether the entire JSF program is necessary. *Bill Sweetman*

X-32A made its first flight on September 28, 2000, and quickly completed simulated carrier-landing tests at Edwards AFB. Once the carrier-landing tests were completed, the X-32A was to be used for "Boeing strategic objectives"—that is, envelope expansion flights which will be measured against sealed-envelope predictions already submitted to the program office. These included a supersonic sortie and in-flight opening of the weapon bays.

The X-32B was undergoing extensive ground tests, focusing on STOVL control software, and was expected to fly late in the first quarter of 2001, starting a 50-flight, 85-hour program that was scheduled to take four months. Early envelope-expansion flights were to take place at Edwards, clearing the aircraft to be ferried to the Navy's flight-test center at Patuxent River. The Navy base, cooler and at a lower elevation than Edwards, was better for STOVL tests.

Lockheed Martin's X-35A flew on October 24 and continued flying envelope-expansion flights into late November, reaching Mach 1.05 on the last flight of the series. The CV-configured X-35C made its first flight on December 16, 2000 and was ferried to Patuxent River in early February 2001 for simulated carrier landings. These tests were completed in early March. The X-35A was modified into the STOVL X-35B, with the addition of the lift fan and thrust-vectoring nozzle. STOVL tests above a grated pit at Palmdale started in February 2001.

Both teams will have completed all other testing before STOVL flights start, keeping their other test aircraft grounded in case it is needed. The teams both plan to approach vertical flight cautiously, starting with decelerating transitions at medium altitude—where there is some space left for a recovery if something goes wrong. The tests will inch toward lower speeds until they are close to a hover. Meanwhile, the teams may fly from the grated "hover pits," making slow translation flights off the pit and exploring the final stages of the vertical landing.

While the flight-test teams approach STOVL in cautious steps, the program managers will complete the final proposals to the Pentagon. The program managers should have evaluated the proposals thoroughly by the time that the competitors are due to have passed the STOVL test. A decision is due in September 2001.

But STOVL is not the only challenge. On December 13, 2000, the long-dragged-out U.S. presidential election ended in a victory for Republican George Bush. The new administration had promised a thorough review of U.S. defense priorities—and certainly would not commit to an effort as vast as JSF before that review was complete.

There is, in fact, a serious possibility that the Bush administration could cancel JSF. Vice President Dick Cheney, in his tenure as secretary of defense in 1988–1992, axed a record number of projects and is unlikely to be impressed by the lobbying of the Marines, who will be the JSF's most ardent defenders. It was the Marines and their Congressional fan club who prevented Cheney from killing the V-22 Osprey in 1990. Ten years later, Cheney is back and the Osprey is still a problem, its production launch stalled as the Marines investigate the second fatal accident in eight months—out of a fleet of 10 brand-new aircraft.

More ominously still, Bush and his defense advisors had spoken during the election campaign about "skipping a generation of weapons." In terms of U.S. national security, they had emphasized the need to develop forces and weapons that would place fewer American service personnel in overseas bases close to conflict zones, vulnerable to attack by missiles or terrorists. They had gone so far as to state a need for "air power—manned or unmanned—that can accurately strike across long distances."

It does not sound like JSF—but it does sound like the sort of airplane that the Skunk Works used to create, and may yet create again.

Chapter 8

MEANWHILE, AT THE SKUNK WORKS...

The Skunk Works never wanted to be famous. Its managers truly believed that it was not always good to work before a large audience, whether in the Pentagon or outside it. Secrecy—and particularly the secrecy that surrounded unacknowledged special access programs or "black" projects—was never aimed entirely at foreign intelligence agencies. It protected the projects from the well-meaning interference of people who wanted a platform for their pet technology or a tool for their favorite mission.

People and organizations who would have felt threatened by a new technology, and may have sincerely believed that it was misguided, were out of the loop. If something went wrong, there were no media or congressional inquisitions to name and shame the "guilty" and discourage anyone else from taking risks in the future.

Paul Martin was a rising Skunk Works engineer in the 1980s, working on the ATF program. He remarked once that, after Lockheed won an ATF Dem/Val contract in 1986, "We had to hold our first meeting in a hangar, because we didn't have a conference room that was big enough. It wasn't fun any more."

In the early 1990s, the Skunk Works became famous. It was a result of several factors. There was the success of the F-117 in Desert Storm. Within

days of the first attacks, the Pentagon released IRADS video of the strikes on central Bagdad. The footage resembled nothing so much as Luke Skywalker's attack on the Death Star in the first *Star Wars* movie—one of the bombs even went straight down a utility shaft.

Next, there was Ben Rich. Razor-sharp and fiercely opinionated, the Skunk Works leader had used his team's mystique during the 1980s as an impenetrable shield against the wrath of the many people he annoyed. (In a bravura performance at a 1987 symposium on commercial supersonic transport, Rich savaged the backers of the National Aerospace Plane, accused them of "conning the president of the United States" and dismissed any commercial use of hypersonic technology as "bullsauce.") Rich was the Skunk Works' chief salesman as well as its leader, and was good copy for print and TV alike.

There was the management revolution. Many companies producing many different products started to emulate the Skunk Works pattern, with small groups of people working on advanced ideas with minimum oversight.

And then there was cable television. Offering the spectacle of flight, the fascination of technology, and the constant presence of risk, aviation makes

DarkStar was designed with two equipment bays, on the right and left lower sides of the body. One held the flight control and vehicle management electronics, and the other contained interchangeable electro-optical and radar sensors. *Lockheed Martin*

Unquestionably one of the strangest-looking flying machines ever built, the Lockheed Martin/Boeing DarkStar unmanned air vehicle borrowed some technology from a much larger aircraft, Quartz, which was never built. *Lockheed Martin*

powerful TV, but could never win the battle for air-time when there were three national networks run from New York (where even a car, critics have observed, is something yellow with a light on top) and Washington-based Public Broadcasting Service, whose producers would sooner be boiled in lead than say anything complimentary about weapon designers. When TV crossed the cable frontier and found vast bandwidth for the taking, the new documentary channels turned to independent producers in Los Angeles, the cradle of both movies and aerospace.

At the same time, Lockheed itself was changing and the business climate was becoming more difficult.

One major change during the 1980s was the steady shrinkage of the former Lockheed-California company. In the days when Lockheed had built F-104 fighters, TriStar airliners, and P-3 patrol aircraft in Burbank and Palmdale, the Skunk Works had been the prototype of the "virtual company." It had a small core of permanent managers and drew staff from its parent company as it needed them. When there was less business, these people would return to the regular company. But as the Skunk Works grew in the 1980s, there were fewer "white" programs at Lockheed in California. A turning point was reached when Lockheed's leaders announced in 1990 that the F-22 would be built at Marietta, Georgia, if the company won the contest with Northrop.

In 1991, the Skunk Works became the Lockheed Advanced Development Company (LADC), a separate unit of the corporation, and subsequently moved from Burbank—a space-restricted site surrounded by suburbs—to Palmdale. Change at Lockheed, however, had not ceased. In 1993, at a meeting that came to be known as "the Last Supper," deputy

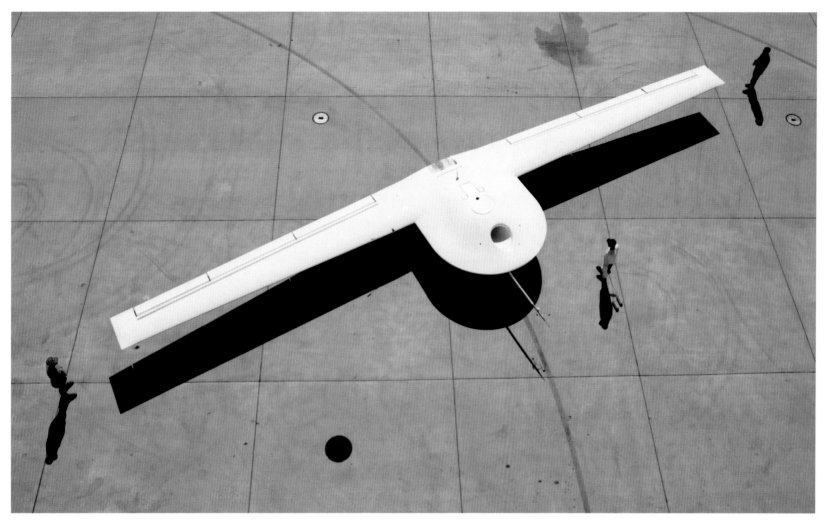

All control for the DarkStar was provided by trailing-edge elevons, using differential drag for directional control. The powerplant was a single Williams FJ44 engine. A low-observable satellite communications antenna was located above the body. *Lockheed Martin*

defense secretary William Perry—the Carter-era godfather of stealth, returning to Washington under the Clinton administration—announced that the Pentagon would no longer sustain as many defense contractors as it had in the past. The message was simple: take over, be taken over, or disappear.

General Dynamics decided to sell its divisions to other companies. Lockheed bought its Fort Worth division—home of the F-16—in 1994. A few months later, Lockheed and Martin-Marietta agreed to merge in what was essentially a takeover by the latter, and the company's headquarters were established at Martin-Marietta's base in Bethesda, Maryland. Renamed the Lockheed Martin Skunk Works (LMSW), the advanced-projects organization was now one isolated division of a very large company, and 2,000 miles from its headquarters. Moreover, many of its sister divisions—including Fort Worth—had their own advanced-projects organizations.

Since then, the Skunk Works has continued to sustain a workforce in thousands despite a remarkable shortage of visible programs. Early in the 1990s, in fact, the organization lost its main new program, a large and highly classified unmanned air vehicle (UAV) known by the code-name Quartz.

Jointly developed by Lockheed and Boeing, Quartz was designed in the mid-1980s as a near-ultimate reconnaissance vehicle. It would have long range and endurance—flying for well over 36 hours at subsonic speeds—and a very high degree of stealth. Instead of just penetrating enemy defenses, it would be able to loiter undetected for hours, gathering intelligence with LPI radar and passive electronic and optical sensors and transmitting it back to the United States via satellite links.

The development of Quartz coincided with the upgrading of Lockheed's RCS range at Helendale to allow it to measure ever-lower RCS

numbers, and with the use of massively parallel computing to solve RCS design problems with greater precision. There have also been persistent reports of new technologies that can reduce a target's visual signature, possibly using large color-changing "electrochromic" panels, comprising thin sheets of light-emitting-polymer material that glow and change color when charged. One such "electrochromic" polymer has been developed at the University of Florida, and is being studied by the USAF as a way of applying a variable tint to the cockpit canopy of a fighter aircraft. In theory, such a coating could also be used over a white-painted skin to vary its color.

Despite a great deal of work—more than a billion dollars over several years—the Quartz project never reached a stable configuration or a single

The wingtip brake-rudder surfaces can be seen slightly split in this view of the second DarkStar. The landing gear location, with the main gears located well aft of the center of gravity, was a contributing factor in the loss of the first aircraft. The second was fitted with a jump-strut nose gear, which extended during the take-off roll. *Lockheed Martin*

Below

With a T-34C trainer flying chase, and framed by a Joshua tree, the second DarkStar approaches to land at Edwards. DarkStar was not a remotely piloted vehicle: the flight controls and vehicle systems were autonomous, and the operator was primarily a mission manager. *Lockheed Martin*

Aiming at ever-lower RCS targets, Lockheed Martin rebuilt its Helendale RCS range in the late 1980s, including this sophisticated target mounting with sloped concrete walls and a retractable pylon, which can lift the model out of a lower-level chamber. Two large sliding panels—open in this view—cover the chamber and close around the pylon (with the aid of airbag seals) during a test run. *Lockheed Martin*

firm requirement. In part, it suffered from having too many chefs—the CIA's Directorate of Science and Technology, the National Reconnaissance Office, and the Air Force all had a stake in the program and had different ideas about operational requirements. It was also technically challenging. The combination of endurance, payload, and stealth drove the vehicle's size upward, and at one point Quartz was projected to have a wingspan of more than 250 feet.

Military commanders would find Quartz information extremely useful—but were skeptical that they would have access to it when they needed it. One of the problems encountered in the Gulf War was that national reconnaissance assets such as spacecraft (and, possibly, classified aircraft) were not controlled by the theater commanders but by high-level Pentagon and CIA organizations. Requests for imagery were slow to be processed at the best of times, and were often turned down

Lockheed Martin's AGM-158 Joint Air-to-Surface Standoff Missile (JASSM) is a collaborative program involving the company's Orlando-based missiles unit and the Skunk Works, which developed its external shape. The composite body uses boat-building technology to reduce costs. *Lockheed Martin*

because the organizations that "owned" the assets did not think that the risks and costs—exposing an air vehicle to being shot down, for instance, or expending maneuvering fuel to place a spacecraft over a target at a given time—were justified. In testimony to a 1995 Congressional panel on secrecy, one senior commander grumbled that classified assets were "pearls too precious to wear."

This was a serious issue with Quartz, because it was a UAV (and UAVs have a far less-than-perfect record of reliability) carrying the most advanced stealth technologies. If the vehicle crashed in denied territory, one source suggested to *Aviation Week*, the USAF would have to send in an F-117 to bomb the wreckage as a security measure.

The AGM-158 has flip-out wings and is sized to fit many aircraft, including the F-117 and the B-2. It uses a GPS/inertial guidance system to approach its target. A nose-mounted infrared camera images the target and compares it to a stored "template." This allows the missile to identify the target and pick a precise aimpoint. *Lockheed Martin*

Future stealth aircraft may be pilotless uninhabited combat air vehicles (UCAVs)—smaller and less expensive than aircraft but smarter than cruise missiles. This VTOL, carrier-based UCAV was studied by Lockheed Martin's Fort Worth division, and uses the same powered-lift system as the X-35: the nose-cone extends forward to open the fan inlet. *Lockheed Martin*

In 1993–1994, the U.S. airborne reconnaissance program underwent an upheaval. A new Defense Airborne Reconnaissance Office, formed to manage UAV programs, identified three "tiers" of requirements, with the high-end Quartz as Tier 3. However, DARO and the Pentagon then canceled Quartz as too expensive and impractical. Instead, the United States would deploy a large, long-range but nonstealthy UAV, known as Tier 2 Plus, and a much smaller and simpler stealthy UAV called Tier III Minus. Because of their Quartz experience, Lockheed and Boeing were awarded a contract to build Tier III Minus without competition.

Sketches of Tier III Minus leaked to the media in early 1995. One publication diminished the impact of its scoop by adding an arrow showing the direction of flight—pointing the wrong way. Later, a Lockheed corporate publication printed the UAV's picture upside down. The confusion was understandable, because Tier III Minus—officially unveiled in

the summer of 1995, and named DarkStar—was one of the strangest-looking flying machines ever built. It resembled a flying saucer with a pair of sailplane wings grafted on to the back, and with a whale's blow-hole on the upper front surface.

DarkStar's shape reflected its mission. For a loitering reconnaissance aircraft with side-looking sensors, it is most important to be stealthy from the side aspect. DarkStar's long, straight wings would generate an RCS spike fore and aft, but it would be easy, in mission planning, to keep that spike away from the target. The saucerlike nose would scatter radiation in all directions, but very weakly, because its upper and lower surfaces were sharply angled away from the vertical. The round-lipped inlet was almost horizontal. There was no vertical tail. The control surfaces comprised a row of movable elevon surfaces on the wing, which could also act as airbrakes and rudders.

DarkStar was a small vehicle, with a single 2,000-pound-thrust Williams FJ44 business-jet engine. It was designed to have an eight-hour endurance, 500 miles from base, and would carry interchangeable radar or electro-optical reconnaissance sensors in a bay on the left-hand side of the body. Imagery would be transmitted back to the ground station by a flush antenna above the short fuselage.

It turned out to be a catastrophic and embarrassing failure. On its second flight attempt, in April 1996, the first DarkStar began its take-off rotation, pitched upward out of control, staggered off the ground, stalled, dropped a wing, and crashed. Flight control software combined with an unusual landing gear design were blamed for the accident. The second airplane did not fly until late 1998, more than two years later, but the entire project was canceled in February 1999.

Otherwise, the only vehicles known to have been built by the Skunk Works in the 1990s are the X-35 Joint Strike Fighter demonstrators and the X-33, a NASA-funded technology demonstrator for a reusable, single-stage-to-orbit space launch vehicle. Lockheed Martin was awarded the contract to build the X-33 in July 1996. Drawing on classified programs from the 1980s, the X-33 is an unmanned triangular lifting-body vehicle with a linear "aerospike" rocket engine integrated into its trailing edge, designed to take off vertically like a rocket and land like an airplane. Most of the body was intended to comprise lightweight composite tanks for liquid hydrogen and liquid oxygen, and the lower surface was to be covered with a metallic heat-shield.

The plan was to start flying the X-33 in early 1999 from Edwards AFB, eventually reaching a speed of 11,000 miles per hour on suborbital test flights. Then, a private industry consortium would be formed to build an operational, two-million-pound orbital vehicle named VentureStar, which would fly in early 2004 and carry astronauts into space in 2006, replacing the Space Shuttle. But major technical problems kept the X-33 on the ground. The liquid hydrogen tanks failed during ground tests in late 1999. Late in 2000 it was announced that the X-33 was not expected to fly before 2003, and in February 2001 NASA canceled the project.

An alternative means of recovering a UCAV to a small ship uses a technique that the Navy tried in the 1950s: tail-sitting. The flight control problems are not trivial—although they are easier to solve than they were in the 1950s—but the vehicle itself is quite simple. No-tail shapes like this are still being studied at Fort Worth for both manned and unmanned aircraft. *Lockheed Martin*

If the Skunk Works has had more successful programs, they have been kept secret. The advent of a new administration in 1992 and the end of the Cold War did not spell the end of black programs. In fact, secret spending in the defense budget, and particularly in USAF research and development and procurement accounts, has stayed high, even though "white-world" budgets have declined.

In its 2001 budget, the USAF planned to spend $5 billion on classified research and development programs. Because white-world R&D is being cut back, this figure is planned to reach a record 39 percent of total USAF

R&D. It is larger than the entire Army R&D budget and two-thirds the size of the entire Navy R&D budget. The USAF's $7.4 billion budget for classified procurement is more than a third of the service's total budget. In 1997, there were more than 150 Special Access Programs, many of them "unacknowledged," or black.

Opposite: Nothing frightens traditional Naval aviators quite as much as concepts like this: a VTOL UCAV operating from a small, stealthy carrier based on the *Sea Shadow* shape. *Lockheed Martin*

A truly extraordinary concept from Fort Worth's UCAV group is a stealthy vehicle that could be launched from a submarine. Concepts such as this are taken seriously by the Navy, which has demonstrated that a submarine can control a UAV and has designed the new Virginia-class submarine to carry unusually bulky vehicles. *Lockheed Martin*

Lockheed Martin withdrew from the first contest to build a UCAV demonstrator, and Boeing produced the X-45A for the DARPA program. Using some X-36 technology, the X-45 will demonstrate the ability to deliver weapons and defeat enemy air defenses, using its own onboard sensors. *U.S. Air Force*

The USAF still refuses to identify its secret flight-test base at Area 51 base, referring to it only as an "operating location near Groom Lake." It is protected from any further disclosure by an annually renewed presidential order.

Area 51's linkage to Edwards AFB is a form of "cover"—actions and statements that are intended to conceal the existence of a black program by creating a false impression in public. The report of the 1995 commission on secrecy concluded that cover was being over-used. While conceding that cover might be required for "potentially life-threatening, high-risk, covert operations," the report stated baldly that "these techniques also have

increasingly been used for major acquisition and technology-based contracts to conceal the fact of the existence of a facility or activity." The report added that "one military service routinely uses cover mechanisms for its acquisition [SAPs], without regard to individual threat or need"

What this means is that the Skunk Works may well have been involved in major classified programs, and that these efforts may be protected by cover stories deliberately crafted to conceal the truth.

However, some information has been published on Skunk Works research that has yet to reach fruition in hardware form. A 1994 patent describes a stealthy vertical take-off and landing (VTOL) special-operations

In addition to working on stealth programs, the Skunk Works launched a difficult effort in 1996 to build a new space launch vehicle. The 100-ton X-33, with a linear rocket motor in its tail, is intended as the prototype for this effort, but was canceled in early 2001 after encountering technical problems. *Lockheed Martin*

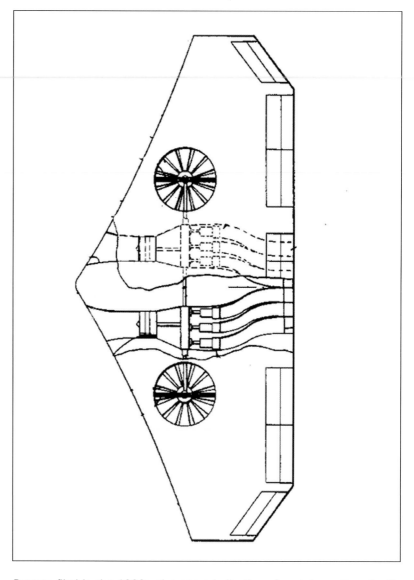

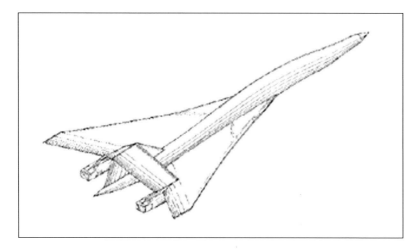

In 1998, Lockheed Martin launched a joint project with Gulfstream Aerospace to develop a supersonic business jet that would not leave a supersonic boom behind it. Although this project has been shelved, Lockheed Martin is still working on low-boom technology under contracts from DARPA. *Lockheed Martin*

Patents filed in the 1990s give some indication of next-generation stealth programs. This is a vertical-take-off special-operations transport powered by six shaft-turbine engines, cross-coupled and linked to lift fans for take-off and landing and cruise fans for level flight. *Lockheed Martin*

Another tailless X-program is the X-44, which NASA plans to base on an F-22 airframe. It could form part of an emerging project to develop an efficient supersonic-cruise aircraft that does not leave a sonic boom. *Erik Simonsen*

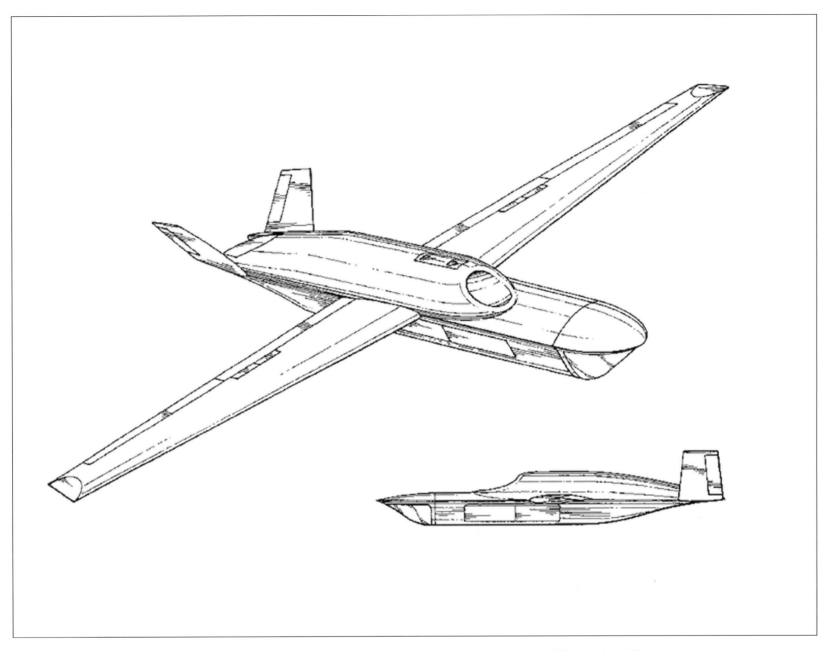

Another new Lockheed Martin design is known as DistantStar, a stealthy long-endurance reconnaissance UAV. *Lockheed Martin*

transport with a six-sided flying-wing planform. The transport would have six turbine engines buried in its wings, driving a lift fan and a smaller cruise fan on each side, and linked by cross-shafts.

Less directly related to stealth—at least at first sight—is the Skunk Works' extensive work on lighter-than-air (LTA) craft. In early 1999, the Skunk Works revealed a few details of a project called Aerocraft, which combined aerodynamic and aerostatic lift and was intended as a transport for heavy military and commercial payloads. Airship Technologies, a U.K. company, was commissioned to build and test a small-scale unmanned model of the Aerocraft (almost 40 feet long).

The Skunk Works has also returned to its work on supersonic-cruise vehicles—specifically, efficient long-range aircraft that produce no sonic boom. This work surfaced in 1998, when Lockheed Martin and Gulfstream announced that they were collaborating on the design of a supersonic business jet. Gulfstream's market studies had convinced the company that a supersonic corporate jet would not be a commercial success unless it could fly at supersonic speed over populated land, while Skunk Works engineers had developed design tools and aircraft configurations that could make that possible.

There is a strong body of theory behind sonic boom suppression. A sonic boom makes a noticeable, annoying, or even damaging noise because the pressure pulse trailing behind a supersonic airplane takes the form of an N-wave. A steep pressure rise caused at the nose of the airplane is followed by a gradual decline to an underpressure, and a steep rise to ambient pressure at the tail. The two sharp rises cause the characteristic double-bang of the sonic boom.

Researchers have suggested that the boom could be mitigated by changing the contours of the nose to create a pressure spike. This seems paradoxical, but the spike creates a local increase in temperature and pressure that increases the local speed of sound and smoothes out the nose shock. The afterbody design can be changed to produce a gentle increase in pressure toward the tail. Meanwhile, the peak overpressure—which affects the boom's total energy—can be reduced by spreading the lift force along the longitudinal axis.

A patent revealed late in 1999 shows a Lockheed Martin low-boom design. Its most unusual features are an elongated nose, with a conical tip, and an inverted-V tail surface that overlaps the wing. The conical nose is intended to create the forward pressure spike. Its sharply swept arrow wing spreads the lifting surface along the vehicle's length. The inverted-V tail may be designed to generate extra lift toward the tail; the inboard trailing edge of a delta provides little lift, but a separate surface can do so.

In late 2000, however, the future of these designs—and the Skunk Works itself—seemed uncertain.

Toward the end of 1999, Lockheed Martin—beset by financial problems and criticized for its management—started to make major changes on its aeronautics side. J. A. "Micky" Blackwell, a former Skunk Works engineer, was ousted as head of the aeronautics sector. Outgoing Skunk Works President Jack Gordon was replaced by an outsider, Bob Elrod from Fort Worth. In January 2000, the company regrouped its aeronautics activities in a new organization headed by Fort Worth—including the Skunk Works, which lost its status as a separate division. Local media reported that "Kelly's Rules"—the 14 commandments of the Skunk Works—had been removed from the walls in Palmdale, and that even the Skunk logo itself was endangered.

Lockheed Martin has been backpedaling since those reports, assuring all and sundry that the Skunk Works heritage will be protected—but the little black-and-white critter was nowhere in sight in the company's pavilion at the Asian Aerospace show in February. In the new corporate structure for the Fort Worth–based Lockheed Martin Aeronautics Company, Elrod was the executive vice-president for programs and acted as "site manager" for Palmdale, which encompassed the Skunk Works and the modification activities that used to be based in Ontario. He also heads a residual Advanced Developments Projects organization. The release announcing the new structure did not mention the Skunk Works once.

By the end of 2000, both the Aerocraft and the supersonic venture with Gulfstream had been terminated. The Skunk Works seemed destined to become at best a UAV shop. Lockheed Martin appeared to be responding to a changed defense-business climate, typified by the JSF program, in which low cost trumped high technology.

But the world may be turning again. The new Bush administration proposes to "earmark at least 20 percent of the procurement budget for acquisition programs that propel America generations ahead in military technology." This budget will be administered directly by the secretary of defense— DARPA on steroids. Such a development might bode well for ultralong-endurance or high-speed UAVs, UCAVs, and new and smaller precision munitions and sensors.

While Lockheed Martin may have pulled out of its Gulfstream deal, it may not stay out of DARPA's Quiet Supersonic Platform (QSP) project, which originated with Lockheed Martin and Gulfstream's lobbying efforts. Recalling DARPA's ASTOVL and stealth efforts, QSP is an ambitious program aimed not just at low-boom technology but at a dramatic improvement in supersonic cruise efficiency, for both civil and military applications.

The story of the Skunk Works, and of stealth, is not over.

The planned follow-on to the X-33 is the VentureStar, designed to lift a shuttle-sized payload into orbit without the aid of solid boosters or an external tank. *Lockheed Martin*